STANDING STARK

Advance Praise for *Standing Stark* by Carla Woody

...Woody teaches us to soar to new heights of consciousness and open magical portals into our Core Selves. Miraculously, she also addresses terrorism, environmental destruction, medical dilemmas and other modern issues that distract so many of us from following our true paths. **Standing Stark** *is a magnificent adventure, as well as a fascinating read!*
—John Perkins, author of *Shapeshifting, The World Is As You Dream It, Psychonavigation* and *Spirit of the Shuar*

Writing from direct personal experience, Carla Woody tackles the mystery of life with sensitivity and an open heart. Most importantly, like an experienced teacher, she probes us to search deeply into the wellspring of wisdom buried in the inner recesses of our being.
—Kyriacos C. Markides, author of *The Mountain of Silence, Riding with the Lion* and others

This book is filled with wonderful stories that help to illustrate with great clarity our underlying relationship with spirit. I'm sure readers will gain insight from Carla's writing, as did I.
—Stephan Rechtschaffen, MD, Co-founder and CEO, Omega Institute for Holistic Studies

Carla's easy, honest style of sharing spins us through this story of a willingness to be fully human—the most sacred act we can ever achieve while being here on earth. She opens her heart to us page after page so that we, in turn, can experience feeling that wondrous gift of being wholeheartedly alive—in every moment—no matter what!
—Jacquelyn Small, Founder, Eupsychia Institute, author of *Awakening in Time* and *Becoming a Practical Mystic*

In **Standing Stark**, *Carla Woody weaves her personal story into a delightful tapestry of self-growth methods and tales of transformation. In reader-friendly language and with a flair for transforming challenging concepts into understandable ideas, Woody describes her unique path toward wholeness and fulfillment. In so doing, she helps her readers discover their own path through the sacred dimensions of life.*
—Stanley Krippner, Ph.D., Co-author of *Extraordinary Dreams and How to Work with Them*

Praise for *Calling Our Spirits Home* by Carla Woody

Calling Our Spirits Home *is truly an enlightening guidebook for anyone looking for directions and tools for expansion, growth and transformation. Carla's gentle words invite everyone on a journey of complete healing and fulfillment. Help yourself with this book and you will find your way home.*
—Malidoma Somé, author of *Of Water and the Spirit*

This is a pleasing and easily read story that tells what we must know and what we need to become to live in this new millennium. It is a spiritual map that offers paths to success in life. Take this book as your map and you will find the way that is right for you.
—Dr. Gay Luce, Founder, Nine Gates Mystery School,
author of *Longer Life, More Joy*

Calling Our Spirits Home *is a beautiful spirit song that gently gathers the dis-integrated, frightened parts of ourselves into the warm unconditionally loving wholeness of a mother's embrace…a celebration of life, mysticism and magic emerging as a blossom from the consciousness of humanity after centuries of growing beneath the compost of an unbalanced, materialist world.*
—Matthew J. Pallamary, author of *Land Without Evil*

Carla Woody writes a fascinating book in which she introduces thought provoking concepts. Her blend of metaphysics, myth and legend is simply amazing. The information in this book is multi-dimensional and gives the reader a chance to discern not only what the "journey" is as it applies to consciousness; it also challenges the reader to do some self-examination…I applaud Woody for being artistic, challenging, and bold in writing this book, and including her personal experiences, lending credibility to her text.
—Metapsychology, The Mental Health Net

STANDING STARK

The Willingness to Engage

CARLA WOODY

Kenosis Press
Prescott, Arizona

STANDING STARK
The Willingness to Engage

Kenosis Press
P.O. Box 10441
Prescott, AZ 86304
http://www.kenosis.net
info@kenosis.net

Cover design: Kim Johansen, Black Dog Design (www.blackdogco.com)
Interior design: Becky Fulker, Kubera Book Design

Library of Congress Catalog Card Number: 2003096771

ISBN 1-930192-02-9
First Printing, USA, March 2004.

All events described in this book are true. Some of the names have been changed to protect the privacy of the people involved.

For Homer

Acknowledgements

Without the involvement of the following people, this book likely wouldn't exist, or at least not in quite the same way, and my life wouldn't be so rich.

I continue to extend gratitude to Don Américo Yábar, who clearly saw my original willingness to engage the journey and has long nurtured me in that process, and to the Andean people who have opened their arms widely in love and called me *waiki*.

Always to my mother and father, Sue and Glenn Woody, I have much appreciation and love. The cocoon of familial support they have unstintingly provided instilled a sense of safety that allowed me to take great leaps into the unknown.

To the folks who repeatedly show up in the forums I offer and create the core that holds the energy of our spiritual community, I have a profound affection and respect. You know who you are. Through all of you, my own learning has deepened.

Many thanks to Jeni Babin and Cindy Foss, my "readers" and *comadres*, who provided concise feedback to the manuscript. I well needed your input.

I also want to acknowledge Marilyn Petrich for her open-hearted ability to be there when needed.

Without Bob Dyer, whose editing expertise provided fine attention to periods, semi-colons and reworking incomprehensible phrases, this book wouldn't be nearly as readable.

*Waiki is a Quechua term for a cherished friend.

Contents

Author's Note

A number of years ago, someone told me that my fate in life is to experience things and then share them with others. It is uncanny how that remark has come to evolve so far. Perhaps it was through that suggestion implanted in my mind—or not. Whatever the origins, the evolution has continued to resonate with me through time, and I live with the prophecy.

This book is a sequel to my previous book, *Calling Our Spirits Home: Gateways to Full Consciousness*. Here I offer you what I have continued to find widespread in the unfolding of spiritual consciousness. Through witnessing my own path and engaging intensively with others, I have found the sweet truth that we are all the same. We are all one at the core. We all desire deeply to go to the identical place. It's only through the choices of our expressions and knowledge regarding possibility that nuances exist.

As for any author, *Standing Stark* is a snapshot of where I am at the time of writing. There are similarities and yet vast differences to my previous book due to the layering effect of my own discoveries. I present to you what I have found to be universal in its essence.

The narrative transitions back and forth through concepts, real-life examples, trance-like metaphor and analogies. This movement is specifically intended. It is meant to take the reader on a ride between ordinary and non-ordinary reality, the conscious and unconscious mind, the literal and abstract. In this way, integration toward true understanding is possible.

During various forums, I am sometimes asked startling questions. They are startling in the sense that they often unnerve a part of me that had been trying to hang onto an increasingly narrow foothold in a reality that doesn't even really occur, except in the limitations of the mind. But I am grateful for the questions because they instill a deeper asking on my part. My intent is that a similar curiosity and affinity for the journey will be transmitted here.

In these pages, I have also related what could be considered paranormal or esoteric events from my own life. Happenings of this nature are by-products of spiritual intent and practice. My sense though is that they present a parallel learning for everyday life. Since all life has meaning to me, I have sought in this text to uncover a relevance from which recommitment to the path naturally transpires.

—Carla Woody

Find sweet music
where you hold tender emotion
— and miss nothing.

Preface

We have heavy rains in Arizona. They normally start in July and go through August. We call the rains monsoons, which may be hard to imagine for those who have not yet experienced the rhythms of the high desert. Sometimes, though, we have a drought year and the rains start later. The tall pines become over-thirsty, beyond being parched. In those times, all of us develop expectancy—trees, plants, animals and humans alike. We are all in it together after all.

But invariably the monsoons come, often with violent storms. Jagged lightning dazzles the sky and thunder cracks so loudly it can bring us up sharply if we're not attuned. In a primal way, we are all more susceptible during periods of scarcity.

Wandering in the forest later, we can see the aftermath. In a sea of towering ponderosas, or their kin, there are those who stand apart. Not frequently, but infrequently, there will be those who are now shed of their needles, their skins laid open by the snaking of a lightning strike. Standing stark, they appear to be dead. They aren't. When I go and put my forehead against their trunks, I feel the elemental filaments that have startled another kind of consciousness within them. Still dwelling in their habitat, they are even more alive than before. They draw our attention—our fascination.

The fire that discharged their coverings often may move to some of the surrounding brush and trees, those in close proximity. Sometimes it may travel from a tree to ignite nearly the entire forest. But before that could happen it was first necessary for that tree to be burned of its own covering before the fire that began with that One could affect its brethren.

We sense that there is something out of the ordinary about those who are struck. At the very entrance to the forest behind my home, there stands One such as this enlivening the passageway into what I have always felt to be a magical place where I go to be washed of my material existence. We have an agreement, this One and I, that I enter a time warp in my walks there—sometimes three to four hours when it seems as though minutes have passed—until I am again clean.

In the middle of the forest, away from usual human evidence, I once discovered a stone circle enclosing a large quartz cross, lying prone. The inside of the circle was carefully tended, the bare dirt swept of debris. The energy and reverence there was palpable, guarded a short distance away by One devoid of its foliage. I return to the circle periodically, taking with me only those who I know will share in the sacredness of that spot.

A number of months ago, some companions and I, seeking refuge from civilization for a few days, were attracted to set up camp in a small clearing in the woods, after searching for somewhere we deemed appropriate to spend a length of time. It was only a few hours later that we realized a magnificent pine was dwelling a few feet away, having met its own sacrifice there. We somehow felt its influence on the peace within that came to each of us after a while.

The lightning strike oftentimes comes suddenly, a bolt unexpected. But there may well be a stirring before the charge and those who have grown the tallest stand most ready to receive.

In order to be ready, we do for ourselves what we know to do as best we can. Yet, there must be no striving. The striving of the material world has no place in this transmission. We need only send our willingness up as a prayer and merely stand waiting. This book is for those souls who hold themselves available—to be struck.

—In the time of monsoons

CHAPTER ONE

Origins

And so we begin, as all human beings do, in space, expressed by a word, permeated by time. Time is a suggestion we swallowed to hold our world together—creating a kind of comfort, but also terror in the false knowing that what passes has a beginning, a middle and an end. We invented words as conductors for experience, but language is meaningless to the intricate nuances of existence. We collectively convinced ourselves that the ground where we stand is solid matter, when the only foundation we truly have we cannot physically touch.

At the soul level, we long to move beyond what is human-made to That which is not. We hope to know the deeper realms of a reality that the everyday eye may have experienced solely through fleeting glimpses—of what it cannot determine. We seek to be promised what we may only have scented wafting through the permeable walls from another dimension. We desire to be inspired by what has stirred our bodies in unknown places with hints of rapture. We ask for the sign when the gift has already been given.

There is an old Taoist story of parents watching their child as she sleeps next to them. In her sleeping state, the child moans and frets. She twists in discomfort. The parents cannot help their child no matter how much she hurts. If the child would awaken, she would see that the suffering is nothing but a dream.

The mind is the charioteer of experience, while the body is the vehicle that carries out the orders of its driver. The gift we have been given is the one called possibility, whose intent offers to tie all together, creating strands of a whole life rather than a disintegrated one. The gift we have been granted is what throws light into dark places. The gift held out to us has always been present. But accepting the gift has a price—courage. It is an undying courage that allows any of us to whip the dream horse and startle awakening.

The Larger Life

Once, during a retreat, I guided the participants through a meditation and afterwards asked each of them to write an archetypal narrative of their individual lives based upon the imagery they had experienced. Through this process, I was fortunate to witness in them shifts of consciousness, tears of release, the dawning of understanding, or even non-understanding, and yet still an opening. While I consider myself a great risk-taker, what I facilitate with others first comes out of my own experience. I *knew* that if these individuals could encounter themselves through mythological patterning and gain a higher perspective, it would touch something that dwells within us collectively.

Some time ago, I went on a backpacking trip into a beautiful canyon. While I had been "car camping" a number of times in the last years, that was my first backpacking experience. I had been cautioned by my companion to pack lightly for the trip since I would carry it all on my back. Every item that went into the pack, or hung from it, involved a mindful decision on my part toward my later comfort. Even so, when we arrived at the place where we finally left the car and I put the full weight of the pack on my back for the first time, I wondered how I would ever make it with the load. I nearly fell over backwards. It took many adjustments before I felt I could carry the weight of my baggage.

Descending the long and rocky, twisting trail, I found I had to be very focused on placing my feet to keep myself upright. After what seemed like an age, we finally reached relatively flat ground and trudged along a path. But it had been a couple of years since my companion had been in the area. Since that time, something natural, or not so natural, had caused the trail he knew so well to disappear. It had been rerouted. He wasn't exactly sure where we were, although he thought we were going the right way. I had been blindly following him — trusting, if you will — while the majority of my attention was taken up with the increasingly uncomfortable burden on my back. I was becoming slightly on edge at the lack of clear direction. Then I became alarmed!

When we rounded what passed for the trail, I realized that if we were to go farther we would have to cross what *looked* to me like a river with nothing more than irregularly placed stones to step on to the other side. While my companion moved nimbly across as though his feet had wings and his back only held a feather, I stood paralyzed. I tried to calculate my path, one stone to the other. All looked perilous to me. I took a step and felt myself becoming even more unbalanced, the heaviness of my burden wanting me to fall backwards and be "swept" away. In the middle of the "river," I couldn't move. I felt terror.

My companion later told me that before his eyes he saw me turn into a frightened child. What I experienced had all the signs of a phobia, previously unrealized. I felt literally glued to the unsteady rock on which I was standing. Without a word and still with an air of respect, my companion came back across the stream and offered his hand to guide me, even putting himself in some danger by leaning far out so that I would feel safer.

This lesser traveled path being what it was, we actually had to cross waters like that two additional times before we came to the campsite he had in mind. Over a particularly dicey crossing, my companion took both of our packs with him at once so that I could make my way in slightly less fear. Needless to say, I felt enormous relief to reach our resting place of a few days, which interestingly enough required yet another stream crossing. In order to hike or photograph in some of the places we went, I still had to make a crossing. Having come over the worst of it, I found that without the heaviness of my pack I was almost able to leap across when I chose.

Eventually, we had to leave and head home. This time, though, the pack seemed lighter to me and somehow more stable. While the food we had carried in was indeed absent, there was something else that had not been present that made the pack seem more a part of me—confidence. So, on the way back when we mistakenly got off the track and ended up walking some distance in a dry riverbed of big rounded rocks, I was merely hot and a little frustrated. I did, however, have my eye peeled for rattlesnakes lurking. When the streams had to be crossed, I traversed them more confidently, only getting a little uneasy once. Even though my companion had warned me that the final hike up the canyon would be arduous, when it actually came it seemed more an act of focused attention.

After we returned to the car and shed our packs, he came to stand in front of me and said, "I wasn't going to say anything while we were down there, but I'm proud of you." Later, when we were driving homeward he asked me if I had gotten any stories for writing during our days out. I had mentioned to him previously that my travels usually brought me most of my writing ideas. I told him then that I wasn't sure. It was only a few days later when it occurred to me that once again I had lived the age-old story and he had been a required part of it. It's a story we all live to different degrees. The challenge we incur is to realize it.

At some time in our lives, we receive a signal to arouse from a deep sleep. If we answer the cue, we set out on a journey toward authenticity that takes us into the unknown. We begin to separate from the selves we thought we were and search for who we are. Along the way, we encounter demons that attempt to derail us. Most often, these demons come when we least expect it and from hidden places. But just when we think we will die in battle, a helping hand appears in the form of a guide. This partnership helps to give us strength. Somewhere along the way, we release something. We find that strength is the mufti that we can wear more and more easily, so that when an unexpected turn takes us deeper into the wilderness, our inner and outer alliances assist us in finding the way. Through this newfound valor, we initiate ourselves. Finally returning home from the journey, we find a community that applauds our courage. It is then this support, as well as inner guidance that allows us to take the next trek.

Re-membering

In *Calling Our Spirits Home*, I laid out the phases of the evolutionary process people tend to go through in their spiritual awakening and continuing travels, illustrating it with ordinary people's stories as examples. It's a model through which I now work with others and call *The Re-membering Process*. The hyphen in *Re-membering* is intended. My sense is that it's the soul's journey in this life to forget almost immediately who we are, become encrusted with society's and our family's of origin programming and then, at some point, to spend the rest of our lives rediscovering our own true nature. This is the universal way of the soul's learning.

To explicitly recount the phases, we must first wake up, or experience a *Sparking*. This arousal state may take place because we realize that we're feeling out of sorts. Something doesn't quite fit. But more often, we're so soundly asleep that the Universe pushes us into wakefulness through such crises as loss of various sorts, or health challenges.

Once we're past the rubbing-our-eyes stage and can look around, we wonder how much of ourselves we had been giving away. In other words, what kind of false life had we been living while being untrue to who we are? We then go through *Separation*. This is a process of detaching from the old self, the one who had been lured into, or opted for, forgetting. At this point, if we are savvy enough, we will begin to question life beliefs we unconsciously ingested. If we truly make it through this stage, we will find ourselves making moves. These changes can be dramatic or subtle. They can cover the gamut from moving geographically to terminating jobs to severing relationships. At the same time, none of these things may happen. The *Separation* may possibly have little outward manifestation and go unnoticed by others. However, an intense discomfort may be experienced inside, enough so that a crack in consciousness begins to occur.

Separation is often a very challenging phase to transition through because everything within ourselves and around us is fighting to keep us where we have been. It's the robust energy of the status quo.

If the core desire to be true to ourselves and live an authentic life is profound enough, it will override homeostasis and propel us into the *Search*. Here we are bent on discovering who we really are and what seems right. In the *Search*, we may move through communities of people and places, a plethora of spiritual traditions, sample various careers and partake of diverse healing modalities. It's a sorting process that begins to give us grounding after the destabilization of *Separation*.

If we perform the tasking well, eventually we will find what rings true for who we are at a core level. When that happens the deepening process of *Initiation* occurs. This is a blessing that we unconsciously or consciously perform for ourselves, recognizing we have found home base. As who we are and what we are about in the world settles in, an integration transpires inside that gives us strength for the next part of the journey.

The *Re-entry* segment is often equally as challenging as *Separation* was. This is the point where we are ultimately aware that we have been through a deepening process, and to complete the circle we must return to the world with our new and more authentic identities. We have gifts to share with others, even if only indirectly through role modeling what is possible. Here we find that most people are too sleepy to notice, or actively turn their backs and refuse our gifts. But once in a while, someone gives a glimmer of interest and perhaps awareness. And we realize that we are sliding back into the world, even if only piecemeal, until we one day find ourselves firmly in place.

The ultimate joke of the journey is that, after a while, we begin to yawn and slip once more into a kind of oblivion. However, the sleep this time isn't so deep and we increasingly arouse from the slumber more easily. Having been over similar ground before, we now carry much more alertness and vigor for what lays ahead in the landscape.

The *Re-membering Process* is not necessarily linear, but within the confines of a model is most easily presented thus. In reality, there is little that is truly linear about human beings. Therefore, we may find ourselves going back and forth between two or three phases, usually only dealing with one or two contexts of life at a time, and we may unfortunately get stuck in the process. But as we are able to complete the journey, even in just one aspect of our lives, it creates an infusion to the Core Self. It transmits a strength and wisdom that allows the peeling away of the layers to become much more fluid than any previous stop/start irregularity. And deep down we *know* this is the path we are meant to take over and over again.

As we choose to plumb the depths of the layering, we sometimes enter an even darker forest. Just because it's darker doesn't mean it's frightening, although it can sometimes be quite unsettling. It's just that the ways through are more hidden, sometimes shrouded intentionally in mystery by the Universe, meant solely for those who persevere toward finding the guidance that will light the way. That's part of the test identifying intent and durability.

We don't meet as many fellow travelers who have opted for this little-worn path. Discernment toward the helping hands proffered may be confusing. Indeed, assistance may even seem invisible or nonexistent. We then know we are traveling the way that leads toward a mystic's life. We must now learn an entirely new form of relating to find the signposts that have been there all along.

The Psyche's Transmission

The impelling momentum of discoveries in the various fields of science in recent years is increasingly bringing that objective field closer and closer into alignment with the subjective realm of spirituality. From the documentation of energy fields and the permeability of all matter to the seemingly endless expanse of the Cosmos, such findings are blowing our tightly held worlds apart with a velocity that creates cognitive dissonance in many.

By focusing on a tiny spot in the far sky, present technology has allowed us to gaze into the further reaches of the Cosmos to countless other galaxies beyond our own. This awe-inspiring look at the vastness of existence can create a real elevation in awareness. It shows the wider mystery beyond religious dogma. It can allow us all to realize, in some ways, what a small part indeed we play in this universe. It can throw into question the very meaning of our individual presences on this plane. It can generate a wider perspective as to the importance that we each place on the mundane worries of our lives. It begs the question of how we may see ourselves as a microcosm of this vast macrocosm. It deals the anxiety: what can we cling to in this grand layering of consciousness?

The questions that come with this newfound awareness may undulate into our psyches and throw the meaning of our lives back in our faces. Within such a grand scheme, we may now taunt ourselves if we had grandiose ideas about making a difference in this world within countless other worlds. With so many possibilities and probable universes, the ultimate trick of our ego selves is to lend us navigation reins toward things we think we can somehow control when it's the role of our higher consciousness to teach us what we cannot manipulate.

What a gift science is to us that it could continually squash all we thought we knew about the nature of reality. Rather than destroying us, it can create much freedom. It could allow freedom from the square inch of our daily lives, which we grasp tenaciously in our fists. It encourages a journey into the much larger existence.

If we set aside religious credos, but examine the common theme across all traditions, especially from ancient eras, we can become aware of the thread that holds strong across space and time. The essence of creation stories and mythologies is the same. These are aspects of human existence that remain unchanged, presented in such ways as Joseph Campbell's *The Hero's Journey* and discussed here through *The Re-membering Process*.

We all have the need to understand why and how we are here. In that effect, scientists are the proselytizers of this new religion called quantum physics. But the responsibility resides with each of us to make sense of it for our own lives. It isn't the role of the quantum physicist to act as the intermediary for our souls any more than it is for any sanctioned holy person to do so. To place that offering at someone else's feet is a cop-out. So, we are left with the question of how to find meaning in universes that are too expanded for the limited ways we use our minds and the dissolution of many centuries' worth of theological indoctrination.

The answer lies with the Core Self and the mythological patterning hardwired into our very DNA. Mirrored time and again in nearly every tale we hear to which we resonate clearly, archetypal guidance is contained within stories and legends throughout time. It is this foundation that we can call upon to provide the valor to continue unflinchingly on life's travels.

It is our own microcosmic journey that gives life meaning and weaves us into the macrocosm of existence. Life *does* begin with each of us. It then expands outward to touch others with *how we live*. The question then is no longer about purpose, but the quality of being and our authenticity within it.

CHAPTER TWO

Beyond Words

I was leading a very mainstream life. While I had some sense of purpose, I additionally had an underlying feeling that something was seriously lacking. Even though there was a recognition of incompletion, I can't say that it was a conscious realization, more of a sense of things not expressed, blocked or segregated.

The previous year I'd left the large government agency where I'd worked nearly my entire career up to that point. Being out from under bureaucratic constraints lent a certain kind of freedom that I craved, but a large part of my livelihood was still generated through that environment where I returned as a consultant. I felt the rigidity of the organization to the point that it triggered an aversion in me.

What I now know is that whenever we have an unreasonably strong response to something external, something is lurking internally of the same nature. At the time, I recognized what I can only describe as flatness, a lack of real engagement to anything in which I was involved. It's unlikely that this fact was apparent to anyone but me. I was known for my mind and abilities for pulling people and projects together. To others, my guess is that I appeared actively engaged in my life. After all, I was busy doing what needed to be done, just like most with whom I came in contact.

But I knew something was omitted. Fourteen years earlier, I'd had a major signal identifying my disconnection. Because of a viral infection that attacked my thyroid, I became extremely ill. I was likely within a hair's breadth of death before I'd had any inkling of the seriousness of the illness. It probably was only through my mother's mother-bear-like, protective attention and demands to the physician I finally visited that I am even alive today.

A major crisis such as this one is often the impetus that will kick start a revelation—or revolution. After my recovery, I finally comprehended the level of absurdity and danger that the lack of awareness of my own condition brought. I was able to discern that I wasn't practicing denial in the sense of not wanting to face something. But more so, I was disconnected from my body to the degree that I had been unable to recognize my lack of health. How could I? My life and level of consciousness was weighted in my head, cut off from my physicality and any real experience or attunement other than mental observation.

I heeded a cry from my Core Self, not even knowing of her existence, and sought out meditation. That was an unlikely avenue back then, only because where I was living at the time offered very few opportunities to explore anything even somewhat resembling consciousness studies. With the help of a couple of books, I put together a practice to which I remained faithful.

Over the years, I found myself becoming increasingly calmer and healthier. I knew that the change was due directly to my dedicated focus on meditation. Indeed, I became much more in tune with my body and its messages to me. I began to trust those messages implicitly, telling me when things were right, or not, in my world.

But I knew something was still missing. I remained an observer to a large degree, not a participant. While I'd read of spirituality and various states that told of that realm, I'd had no direct experience. I intellectually knew that Spirit was an aspect of my makeup, but couldn't quite grasp even the concept of such a reality. And yet there was something underpinning my entire existence that called out for this wholeness. Some part of me deeply desired integration.

When strong intent is present, the means to fulfill it will automatically appear. But I didn't know this truth at that point in my journey. I only knew that I felt somewhat fragmented, and one day noticed an ad in a professional journal for a retreat with a Peruvian shaman to be held in the Southern Utah desert. Ignoring the fact that my sole idea of camping then was in pensions in large European cities, or that I didn't even know what the term "shaman" meant, I felt a strong draw in my body to call and register. So, I did.

Four months later, I flew cross-country to Salt Lake City where I was picked up with some other retreat goers and driven some hours south to a remote canyon in the San Rafael Swell. The beauty of the area was incredible and helped to overwhelm my uneasiness of being with people with whom I wasn't acquainted, and an upcoming event about which I knew absolutely nothing.

When we finally rolled into the makeshift camp, I climbed out of the truck feeling a mixture of excitement and apprehension, the two being closely linked anyway. While in this state, I noticed a brown-skinned man making his way toward me. He had dark, wavy hair, a mustachioed, handsome face, and wore a woven poncho. His eyes sparkled. He smiled broadly and wrapped his arms around me in greeting. As he did so, any fear I felt dissipated immediately and was replaced by great warmth swelling from some place inside me, unlike any I'd ever felt. This was the man the sponsors had advertised as a shaman, the person who, in the years ahead, I would come to know not only as a mystic and teacher of the heart, but a cherished friend—Don Américo Yábar. My meeting him was to change the fabric of my entire life. And I had asked for it unknowingly.

Around the campfire that evening, Don Américo introduced the subject of intent through his translator. He encouraged each of us to set our intent that evening for the week that was to follow. I went off on my own to think about what he'd said, the whole idea of intent being a slippery one, at best, that I had a challenge grasping. However,

13

I decided that I must have set my intent, at some level, before I even came. That was what pulled me to the retreat not even knowing what it entailed. I wanted to be joined. I wanted direct engagement. I wanted integration of my mind, body and spirit. I told no one.

The next morning held the usual gorgeous, blue desert sky. The group had hiked some distance from our camp and found a natural rock amphitheatre. We made ourselves comfortable in the shadows of the boulders, out from under the Utah sun which was already getting quite warm. Don Américo began to speak. I don't remember now exactly what he said. I was being lulled by the lilting rhythms of his and his translator's vocal patterns that took the meaning of the words to some unconscious level.

Suddenly, he stopped and gazed intensely at me. He motioned for me to come to the middle of the circle where he stood. Under normal circumstances, I would have done so reluctantly, if at all, not being comfortable "exposing" myself to others in that way. In that case, however, I felt completely at ease.

I approached him. He stood directly in front of me only about eighteen inches away, his liquid brown eyes locking onto mine. It was as though he was channeling pure love directly into my being. Both of his hands hovered right outside my body at the chest level.

Making a motion of pulling apart outside the heart center, he said, "The way to *see* is with the body's eye."

I felt what I could only describe as a sweet welling in that energy center that began to undulate, creating a rippling effect.

He moved one hand up to my forehead. Making a wiping motion in my subtle energy field, he proclaimed, "*Not* the mind's eye!"

I felt something shut at that level, all the while the heart energy continued to reverberate. I was unaware of anything other than large waves of effervescent warmth that seemed to echo silently, returning from the stones surrounding us, further intensifying the awakening. People seated around us gasped and murmured. I have no idea how long I stood that way. I do not know how I found my feet to return to my seat. I do not recall what occurred the rest of the day.

I was opened. I was filled. I'd had my first direct experience—beyond words.

Substitution

Words are the shell. They feed intellectual knowledge. What lies in the middle of words is the seed that, if presented and embraced in a certain way, will take us to the place we seek. But words in and of themselves are worthless, like so many knickknacks we may collect and leave on a shelf to gather dust, if we are unable to move beyond them.

For the purpose of making a point, I'm going to offer a distinction between hearing and listening. We'll regard hearing as the mechanical process of sound hitting the apparatus that then filters through to register in our brains; within whatever paradigms we've already developed. The brain quickly sorts the sound or series of words into what appears to be the relevant slot in order to determine logic. However, when something is boxed in, other things are locked out.

Listening is the process whereby we are able to admit a further awareness than the one first taken in through the sonar signal. Listening actively ignores cognitive dissonance, if there is any, to see *how there may be* relevance—instead of involuntarily determining *how there isn't*.

After all, if we're on the spiritual path, we can trust that there is much we don't know. These mysteries are hidden from us until we are ripe. The paradox is that we frantically attempt to know in order to surrender to the place of not knowing! The other paradox is that there *are* no mysteries because the cues are surrounding us all the time. We're just too tied up to recognize them.

In order to be open to the deeper awareness, the possibility resident in the word-seed, we need to be in a state of receptivity.

Instead, we more often take the words, and through our limited education, create conjectures that lead to certain expectations of what is meaningful, good, right and true.

Expectation is related to control. Control is related to fear. When we control, through convoluted strictures, the nature of our comprehension, we merely exhibit our fear. Our fear-based, narrow understandings are released through the mind like so much perfume, and we only notice what we expected coming back to us through the attraction of what we emit. In this way, we generate our own limited happiness, disappointment, sadness, anger, confusion and general heaviness. We perpetuate this process automatically—unless we consciously seek to break the cycle.

Too often when a spiritual teacher is speaking to a group, I have seen some of those present scribbling furiously in notebooks or journals, thereby splitting their attention. How can we write and really listen at the same time? I have also heard people ask a plethora of questions, or make comments, most often having little to do with the real depth of the words given.

Those are times when I've witnessed hearing. In many who only hear, there's a quiet desperation. It's a desperation coming from the Core Self, who in silent times, will receive the meaning, or transmit something already deeply known. The problem is when the logical mind is too busy with internal slotting and chatter. Openings rarely exist. Little or no space can appear for something other than what has already been categorized and catalogued!

These are often the same people who are also immediately on to the next thing without time for integration. Therefore, no mastery is possible. The compulsion is generated because they didn't quite get "it" in previous talks, classes and retreats they attended, or books they read. Anxiety is the overt driver, while deep desire is its foundational engine.

I readily understand this urgency and desperation through the years of my own disorientation. I painfully remember the intensity, frustration and seeming hopelessness of trying to reach out to something that has no tidy form. And yet, somewhere inside those of us who have a strong commitment to the deeper life, a profound tenacity exists. We keep reaching for what will touch us and reassure us of our own Divine Presence in the face of nothing seen or felt.

In reality, all we need to *do* is sit in silence and allow the space for immersion and emergence. This is the perpetual school. We won't be asked to regurgitate facts! There are no facts in this context anyway. We are asked to learn and allow the knowing to then inform our expressions. Otherwise, we are merely parroting shallow platitudes because the seed has not been planted, but remains dormant on the surface.

We don't really learn until we receive it in the body, in conjunction with the mind and the energy of the spirit. In order to do so, we only need listen and the essence, the real resonance of the teaching, will implant itself. We don't have to worry that we will forget, that we won't be able to call it up on demand. It will be there—at the level where it makes a difference.

It won't be there if we don't allow ourselves to be present. Rather than frantically scratching down every word, we need only jot down a phrase or two, if anything. Then, at a later time, we can recall its resting place wherein we embody it. We can sink beneath the words through the state of being we originally experienced in the moment.

There's a reason that Jesus taught in parables, as did many other masters. Storytelling is a way to skirt around the logical mind that has a tendency to throw up roadblocks to things that seem out of the ordinary to its usual reference shelf. The deeper mind takes to metaphor joyfully, sorts it in ways to find the timbre of its own truth for the Core Self. And nothing of untruth can find a resting place. In some ways the cataloging process is not so different from the logical mind. The differentiation is in the methods used for schooling those things seen and unseen, known and not known, normal and paranormal.

Translation

We hear words and sink into silence. And we start from silence and arise through words. It is within this natural cycling that profound works have historically emerged, not only to create a statement, but to provide a shift in the culture and spiritual life through the ages.

It's highly unlikely that Picasso's *Guernica* came to him through hearing. It issued through listening. Anyone who has ever seen this mural depicting the Spanish Civil War has to be deeply moved. It comes from a cry of the spirit; so much so that at the time I saw it many years ago, the curators still found it necessary to protect the painting from attack by the dictator Franco's supporters long after he passed. It was housed alone in an annex to the Prada Museum in Madrid. Spectators could see it only by viewing it from behind a guardrail and through a wall of glass standing about ten feet in front of it. Nevertheless, for those who listened, it evoked intense emotion.

Just the same, I sat one time talking to a friend who was a wood-crafter, living in France at the time, about his art form. He related to me how he would sit with the wood, touch it and even stroke it. Once he'd done that he had a sense of what wanted to emerge—from the wood and from him. Michelangelo spoke of a similar process with marble.

There's a time to move beyond the knowledge traditionally taught to knowledge experientially found. During one of my Sunday Salons, a discussion forum I sponsor, where the subject of this chapter was the topic, two participants, who work as speech therapists, discussed what operating through deep connection brought to them—and to the autistic children with whom they worked.

One spoke first and said, "I truly have to get out of all my training, whatever we're taught. When you're with a child who is totally unintelligible, it makes no sense to try to speak in the typical way. It's better just to be quiet, watch and listen, to just be with them and have an experience of who they are. I get a lot more language that way, even though it doesn't sound like what we're used to hearing.

"As soon as I go into my head to all my training, I don't get as much communication or connection with the child. When I just hang out with them, it's not so much about the English language, but an inner language at that point."

The other woman added, "You think about this child. What are you going to do with this child the next day at school? If you just stop thinking about it, trying to plan, and just go in there and be with the child, it works! I mean, things happen!

"I've often said of myself, I'm not a good teacher to other therapists because I can't explain things that I do with kids! I go to the workshops and hear all this good stuff, but it's not ingrained in me. But I go in with the kids and things happen!

"(Teachers may say) why did you do that? I don't know! It's just what I'm supposed to do."

They both agreed that it's not about doing, but about being. The first therapist summed it all up. "I just brought a tray of shells in one day. I got more of an experience of the kids. I didn't bring a pencil. I didn't bring anything to record. I was amazed at how much I saw and heard in a different way. I learned a lot more about how they really want to connect and communicate.

"We're so trained to do these techniques. But ultimately when you get mastery at what you do, it's about letting go. There are tools we use, but it's not really about any of that. Those tools aren't really about what makes us good therapists."

There is a very real element about words getting in the way oftentimes, along with the rigidity of any structures we've been taught. If we would just surrender to the quiet, what we need will be there to guide us, whatever our focus.

We all need an expression that emerges from our listening, whose truth bubbles up through our allowing. The allowance can then take shape as an art form. It doesn't matter the form. It could be gardening, sitting counsel with a friend, holding a child—a life's work. Anything that evolves by listening, informing the mind through the whispers springing from the word-seed qualify as the Divine art. It's grace issuing from secret passion.

Direct Knowledge

Deep listening activates the faculties beyond our five senses that most of us don't commonly use. When we have our ears on and our eyes and hearts open, we're alert to synchronicities and follow the cues if that's what is offered. We feel subtle energy, our own and that of those around us—and we *see* beyond what is presented on the surface.

The first time *seeing* happened for me in an obvious way was during a seminar I attended. I had been in a trance-like state listening to the speaker, allowing his words to drench me. When the talk was over, the remnants of the state remained. People were milling around and talking. I was one of them. Suddenly, it wasn't their words I heeded, but something else. It was as though a hand had spontaneously reached in and plucked off the mask of their words. I *saw* everyone, their personalities exposed beyond doubt. Every way I turned, I *felt* people through their energy fields. It was at first overwhelming, it being so strong and new. Through a profound synesthesia, I experienced the warmth of one, the inflexibility of another, the hope of yet another. None of my observations had anything to do with what any of them were saying.

All was there. Nothing was hidden. It never is. But we normally rely on words. It was this same kind of *seeing* that let Don Américo immediately know of my fearful state when I first entered the campground and met him in Utah. He sent me the energy of his heart by enveloping me in his arms, relaxing me. It followed that my fragmented state was clearly visible to him, even though I told no one of my intent toward integration. He just *saw* me. What he did wasn't magic. He merely attuned to the reality beneath the surface. We can all learn to do the same.

If we listen, instruction comes to us in times of crisis, finding the opening between the words of habit and disbelief. During Sunday Salon, a man spoke up and told of a time when he'd been lost in the forest.

"It was a very anxious moment in my life. I thought I was going to rot there. It was in the winter and I wasn't properly dressed. It was getting dark. I kept wandering around for hours. I called out in desperation.

"And then I had an insight. I asked myself a question, 'How long have you been studying *A Course in Miracles*? The answer was, 'For a long time.' I realized that I had to get quiet and listen for that inner voice. And I did that.

"It wasn't audible, but it was a direction. If I'd go over the hill on my right, everything would be okay. And don't you know that at that moment my ego came out! Questioning the direction! But I put that on hold and went over the hill.

"There was a public restroom up there! I thought, 'There must be some civilization.' And sure enough, a ways from there was a playground and a road. I had to test the direction on the road because it was dark. Again, I was told to go to the right.

"I finally came up on the highway! That time held a profound message to me. Just be quiet."

Residing in the Garden

We move out of the Garden when we voice what does not arise from our own Divine Heart. There's the evolution of learning, but we've got to come to a place of discovering our own authority and trust it. When that happens we know we have been initiated through direct experience. That's why no one else can truly initiate us except perhaps as recognition of our path, or to assist in gelling a commitment. But *we* still make the commitment. Once initiation matches direct experience, we can move through Re-Entry of the Re-membering Process. We then bring home our Core Identity intact—not someone else's.

The Divine Presence we discover within ourselves is not a space of words. Words are a poor substitute for the warm, blissful silence. If the truth be known, we are all able to discern when we begin and end in that place. We *know* it and it's unmistakable. There's a transmission we receive from that innermost place that shapes the words we speak. Then, it's not the words so much as the energy infusing the things we say or do that trigger our own deepening as we witness ourselves, and touch the emptiness in others. In this way, the inside meets the outside and the paranormal becomes normal.

CHAPTER THREE

The Inner Point

You have probably seen Japanese paintings largely consisting of a vast sky, mountain, or even a waterfall with really nothing else but a small object such as a person or an animal somewhere in the very lowest region of the painting. A painting of this nature may appear to have little distinction of any sort to an unschooled Western eye. Indeed, we may not be interested at all. But the Japanese artist is making an important statement that we could well take as an aphorism. This particular type of work is called a "one-corner painting." In this genre, the object is carefully considered and meticulously placed in a space where it will influence the environment contained within the work. This is where we might take notice of the message this style of painting holds. It's really a question of influence and its source. Who or what is the actor?

There is a ritual in which some of us may engage to instill hope for the future—the New Year's resolution. We make goals toward such things as better health, smoother relationships, adjusting careers or money matters. Our culture drives objectives and results. If we're not *doing* something and *getting* results we laid out for ourselves—or that others have put in front of us—then something must be wrong with us. At least, this is what we're told by the voices in our heads, or by family, bosses or friends. Yet, goals and objectives—*getting* and *doing*—are merely the surface layer of a much deeper structure existing within us. It also tells the story of our internal processes and how married we are to a state called frenzy.

If we are plowing the road toward authenticity, we can begin to recognize that something else has begun. The goals and actions are still there, but they have loosened. Perhaps we have even begun to have some confusion about who we are—if anyone, what we are doing—if anything, and where we are going—if anywhere. Something seems out of kilter, not quite enough or too much.

At this point, we may tend to throw ourselves into even more activity. *Harder* and *better* will surely get us to the place of comfort again, and we find it doesn't. Life just gets more fragile until the layers become so thin that we have a breakthrough in spite of ourselves.

If we're one of the wise ones we will instead recognize a *stirring*. Of what we're not sure, but if we know enough to become silent and still, a resonance will begin to emerge. Rather than thrust aside the discomfort of something unfamiliar, we can gladly go into it. Much as we find that if we immerse ourselves into a physical pain and let go of contraction, we discover an interesting fluidity and the distressful edges dissolve. If we allow the flow to expand, we can make room for what is actually quite familiar, but usually forgotten somehow—true intent.

Dichotomy of Mind

Intent is to intention as expectancy is to expectation. Intention *tries*. Intent *is*. We've all heard the phrase about a road being paved with good intentions. How many times have we said to ourselves, "That's not what I intended?" That means we missed the mark somehow, particularly from an expectation we may have had. Expectation is a very tight answer, a very little box. Many opportunities are missed when vision is so narrow as to limit the outcome and the actor is asleep to a wider existence.

Intent is an inner point of light—that coherence of clarity and possibility—that we travel to only by clearing debris obstructing the chamber doorway. Intent is that place that can't truly be named and can only really be spoken of indirectly in metaphor or drawn through symbolic imagery. But those who have dwelled there know the boundary-less sensation She brings. From intent, we experience unstinting expectancy. Expectancy is the trust that produces increasing instances of right fit, which then are given to right action. Intent is the attractor. Expectancy is the fulfillment.

It's equally true that intention is the attractor and expectation the fulfillment. It depends on what our focus is. Consider an astronomer. An astronomer must learn how to use a telescope with clear precision for observing deep space. While focusing on the chosen area, any unsteadying of the instrument by the slightest bit of disturbance and the sight piece will be moved. Therefore, the intended target will be missed altogether. The view will be shifted. On the other hand, if the astronomer possesses an inner precision, through a pinpoint in time, a field of endless galaxies may be discovered.

The great traditions speak of intent and expectancy in various ways. In the Tao Te Ching, *Tao* is Absolute Reality. *Te* is how Absolute Reality manifests. From the Jewish mystics, the force of Creation is known as *Shekinah* and the Greeks know this wisdom as *Sophia*. Sophia beckons and welcomes merging, just as the Hindu tradition teaches *yoga*, which means "union." But this can only happen if we get beyond what we have ingested—on numerous levels.

Dwelling Places

The doorway and ladder are ancient symbols. One is for the threshold we must cross; one for the ascension we must make. What they both hold in their archetypal meaning is opening. Sometimes the door seems so heavy and unmovable, we find it necessary to slip through its cracks. Not so strangely, the rung of a ladder we thought so secure breaks. We find we must step over to the next rung, or find another ladder. As we find more ways than the ones we thought we knew, something opens widely within us. And that freedom takes us to the place we seek.

Sixteenth century mystic Teresa of Avila used the metaphor of the seven dwelling places within a castle to describe the trek through the multiple rooms of existence we are proffered. Strangely, there is an uncanny validity to her teaching that parallels present life, perhaps even more so than during the time she lived. Or, it just proves that the essence of our individual challenges essentially stays the same as does human nature. It's merely a question of complexity.

What follows next is a metaphoric interpretation of the journey through the doorway and into the innermost chamber of the interior castle—a path that is already well known to the Core Self.

The Admission Ticket

Right away there's the consideration about being inside or outside the castle walls. It's not only about being outside the walls. There is also a moat to cross and sometime dangerous guardians to confront to gain access through the massive entryway. If there are guardians, then you can just about guarantee that what is hidden behind the walls must be precious. But those who are outside the walls are asleep to what the hidden treasures might be.

Their only level of attention is survival in the basest sense, how to try to manipulate the material plane to ensure their own continuity and derive sensual pleasures in the process. There's nothing wrong with enjoyment of the senses. In fact, it's part of being human. It seems true, though, that when it's done outside the castle walls where the focus is so narrow, the pleasuring is likely trying to feed something devoid of filling. When you awaken to this understanding, you realize that you are living outside an apparently inviolate sanctuary. The protective trenching appears deep, the castle doors thick, the castle walls high and the guardians vicious.

What you must come to realize is that these are illusions of your own making. The sanctuary is open to all. But there's a price. You must be willing to brave the piranhas swimming the moat of intention. You must do so even while you continue to hand-feed them with the doubts of your own making that nourish them and allow them to multiply. As you match the task, you then will find that the protectors of the castle walls are gargoyles who merely mirror back to the exterior world the image of their own grotesque mask. You can then recognize the gargoyles for the sweet spirits they are and claim your admission ticket to the castle.

Having gained entry, you can still hear Teresa's fleeting whisperings resonating through time, promising the divine inner chamber where Sophia resides. But it's not yet evident to your unadjusted eyes. There's no hall that gives the impression of providing a direct passage. It's more a series of staggered rooms, perhaps eventually spiraling awkwardly toward the interior. You're asked to have faith. In this faith, you're asked to close the castle door to the outside and step into the First Dwelling Place.

The First Dwelling Place

In the middle of the First Dwelling Place, there's a soft glowing candle sitting on a flat stone, held upright by a pool of its own drippings. You were told by a gargoyle upon passing through the threshold of the castle entryway that each room would contain a practice, as well as other purveyors of focus. The key to each progressive Dwelling Place would be found in the discovery and consistency of right attention. The gargoyle had intimated in a barely audible voice, "It's not the content. It's the process." But the message was then too subtle for your denser nature, being so newly arrived from outside.

You did remember the words about attention, though, and found your eyes drawn to the flame of the candle. The flickering of the taper and its golden aura mesmerized you until you found yourself being pulled inside your mind, as though the fire had something to do with you—what was resident within. And just for a brief moment you found a still place, a slight glimpse of self-knowledge.

But then an unknown wind nearly extinguished the spark and caused a flare to dance upon what had been in the background, allowing it to now proceed to the foreground. Myriad thoughts began clamoring for your notice. There was the car payment to be made, the boss to be appeased and the next sale to be closed. Then to feel good, there was the new outfit to buy for the party on Friday and wondering what was wrong with a friend, which must be your fault because you weren't there when needed. Or, you weren't paying attention because your children were shouting in your ears, fragmenting your attention, futilely attempting to encompass all detractors.

The gargoyles did the best they could to ferret out the furor, but you often bring with you inside what was lodged outside, like so many fleas hopping on your shoes for a free ride. Yet there was the flicker of the flame, an invitation mostly ignored but sporadically remembered—in the First Dwelling Place. And when you remember to engage the light more often—at least with your eyes if not your heart—then you can see something . It's a crack in the stone, almost obscured by the hardening pool of wax spreading out from the candle. You realize then that if you allow your mind to melt into the candle's fire you can become like so many drippings seeping through the fissure of time leading to the Second Dwelling Place.

The Second Dwelling Place

You then find yourself in an oak-paneled room with plenty of cushy old club chairs drawn companionably around a fireplace so large that you could stand up in it. The walls to either side of the fireplace, and to its right angles, are comprised of floor-to-ceiling bookshelves. Lining them are nearly all the words ever written, bound in pages, containing attempts at translation of the true nature of existence.

You discover that you are becoming overwhelmed because there is so much there. You observe an inadequacy in your education. You don't know where to start tutoring yourself. But you detect that direction is given. A book is pulled out slightly so that it would stand apart from the others in their tidy rows. You automatically notice it then and pluck it from its storage place.

Another one strangely falls off the shelf on its own to land at your feet. You bend over to pick it up and carry these treasures over to one of the club chairs where you discover other chronicles magically awaiting you, stacked haphazardly. As you immerse yourself in the written word, you begin to take in countless conjectures and perspectives about reality you heretofore had not considered. And it becomes so confusing, given what you thought was true.

You feel ungrounded and isolated in your new knowledge. You wish there were those who would be willing to explore further with you, and even commiserate on falsehoods by which you may have been living. As you hold this wish in your head, you find people drifting into the room, milling about the shelves, settling into chairs, warming themselves at the vast fireplace. As natural groupings emerge, you notice that some fall into quiet or excited discussion. Others expound as though from a pulpit, while still others sit silently together. You find yourself poking your head into one enclave and then another; sometimes listening, at other times contributing and yet other times just being present.

Indeed, you experience the latter to be the most unfamiliar to you. Just as you realize the quiet comfort of that state, the ringing of a cell phone splits the air and some fools start using remote controls to flip through channels of the televisions lining the back wall, previously unnoticed. Below the televisions, computers boot themselves up as though by an invisible hand. The din becomes quite noxious amid the pollution emitted from digital screens, pagers and pulpit pounders.

You bear witness to small groups drawing closer to further isolate their circles of quiet inquiry and the meditators building walls of energy to provide separation. But you also notice increasing furrows of irritation on various brows and eyes glancing over shoulders. You somehow know they are being seduced by awaiting e-mail or the next reality series on television, frantic that they might miss some tasteless event, like yesterday's soap opera. You know this because you find the same distractions yourself as your own critical internal dialogue kicks in—telling you how you're wasting your time seeking a wider model of the world, what you *should* be doing instead and exactly *how* you should be doing it. Until finally you reach a crescendo where you feel buffeted back and forth between two polar existences and scream in silent rage: *where is sanctity?*

Here in the Second Dwelling Place, your *real* trials are first introduced. You thought you had trials before, but that was the mundane world. The trials resident herein are a battle for consciousness undertaken with equal zest by what you conceive of as both sides, or dualities. When you've stared with intensity at an image composed of opposing hues for a length of time and look away to another space, you will find the after-image still present, now superimposed upon where you had wished to direct your attention. Thus, it serves as an enticement to look back to where you were previously, even while you want your focus to stay stable on the desired target.

As true, when you give in to enticement and look back, you still hold the after-image of the place of your desired concentration. You suffer through an unrelenting tension of what you qualify as opposites. As you are jerked and batted about, *any* gain on your attention being the prize, the stress creates static electricity that pops open a hidden panel inside the fireplace revealing a secret passageway—to the Third Dwelling Place. Even though the fire will graze you, you willingly dart into the darkness beyond, hoping to escape this madness. And you do—for a while.

The Third Dwelling Place

You realize you are descending rapidly as you follow a dank tunnel, until you begin ascending again. You come to the end of the passageway, but look up to see a circle of sky some dozens of feet above through an access hole. You climb the ladder appropriately provided and pop out into a small courtyard containing all manner of flowers, soft grass upon which to lie and a huge tree against which to rest your back. You realize that you have just come through a mock well, fittingly camouflaged. What a sweet relief to be in such a place soaking up some gifts of nature!

You breathe in the heady scents of blossoms, which transmit their smells directly to the limbic brain, accessing pleasing memories. Mesmerized, you fall headlong into a simpler time in childhood when you sank into warm grass, bees circled lazily looking for pollen, butterflies flitted around butterfly weed, and you watched the clouds travel by taking on one animal form and then morphing into another. As you access that time long past, you find you are there once again.

Lying on the moist ground, gazing at the sky, becoming enveloped by the sounds and smells of nature, you begin to lose yourself. You become boundaryless and merge with everything and nothing at the same time. You have a long-forgotten experience of unity that leads you to remembrance. You know in this moment what is real and what is not; what is important and what is not; who you are and who you are not.

Because you ache from the recollection of your perceived separateness, you vow to instill practices that will take you frequently to this place of merging. Because you are reminded of your true nature, you promise to spread your gifts. And due to your experience of timelessness, you affirm the time in your current material reality.

In the same moment, you become critical of those who do none of these things. Or they do them "unsuccessfully." Or they don't do them according to the way you do them. You can direct ill thoughts equally toward yourself. And spiritual egoism is born even while you seek to be *without* ego or attachments.

Now, to test your commitment to the trek inward, you call tribulations upon yourself—a job loss here, a relationship soured there. Never mind others' attachments. What about your own? Will you retreat? Will you hang on? Will you cry with anguish?

Only rarely will you realize that the tests are of your own making, brought on by the niggling doubts in your mind reaching out to fulfill a match. Only *if* you realize that this is the case, will you be transported up into the clouds and then coughed out like so many raindrops—to the Fourth Dwelling Place.

The Fourth Dwelling Place

You land with a gentle thud. Your eyes pop open. Not being completely conscious for the trip, you don't know quite how you got here. Get here you did, though, and you take in your sparse surroundings. You seem to be in an interior room. You sense it as a tower room of some sort, fairly removed with high ceilings.

But you have no evidence since there don't seem to be any windows or doors. The walls are covered with heavy tapestries, absorbing any outside sound. As well, the floor is thickly carpeted. Discovering your feet to be bare, you bury your toes into the deep softness, feeling comforted in the silence. There are overstuffed pillows strewn on the floor and a few caftan-like robes folded neatly over a ladder-back chair. The chair sits in front of a scrubbed wooden desk; pen and paper await on its surface. A little distance away stands a set of bookshelves. There are a few books there, but not many. More so, there are reminders from your everyday life—photos of family and friends, the cat's toy, a phone number on a piece of paper, a small calendar with appointments scratched in the appropriate dates.

There are those reminders, but you find more attraction to the idea of donning a robe and sitting upright on a pillow. You follow the attraction. After you adjust your body, stretching the places that need loosening, you follow your breath to an interior space. But this time it's different. There's not quite the striving for quietude. Oh, the mind chatter is still there. But you only occasionally find yourself taken off on a rabbit trail by some stray thought. When it happens, you notice it and come back to the breath. There's not at all the angst with which you sought this vicinity before. You have a kind of patient anticipation.

In this expectancy you find movement, with an ethereal quality that touches you in the way that nothing ever has. A vision comes that is beyond anything you could imagine and a disembodied finger reaches out and anoints you with aromatic oil at the Third Eye. You *feel* its feathering touch even as the warm smell of sandalwood enters your nostrils. Even though you're not sure of the meaning, you know it's a transmission of some sort.

In this moment you have a profound learning—the difference between *knowledge* and *experience*. And you know that infused prayer, holding yourself from a space of intent, is the offering that takes you there. Your heart stirs and you literally feel a shimmering in the middle of your chest. This new sensation obliges you to raise yourself and walk to the desk, to sit down and to write. As you write of your experiences, you glance over at the reminders of your commonplace life and your heart swells even more for who you are and who travels with you. The penning of your encounters takes you deeper and deeper into an abode you previously didn't even know existed—the Fifth Dwelling Place.

The Fifth Dwelling Place

It's an abode of formlessness of a sort. If you look down, you have an occasional glimpse of your feet, hands or torso. Even though you know you exist in physical form, the need to hold onto that container is considerably lessened. You have a sense of its purpose now, as well as that of the words and imagery of your days, thoughts and feelings swirling around you. As with so many artifacts sitting on the altar of your unfolding, you can fondly cherish the return to which they have brought you.

Life is no longer a duality, but more like one of those pictures that tests you to determine if you see *either* the face *or* the urn in the same image. Here you encounter the ability to hold both in your awareness at once. From this point, it becomes an almost automatic transition—to the Sixth Dwelling Place.

The Sixth Dwelling Place

And you find yourself splashed like rich red wine into the pineal bowl of the Holy Grail. Swimming in this warming liquid, your palate acquires a taste for what is resident here and you become the willing betrothed awaiting the Divine marriage. The desire to merge is overwhelming even though you know that matrimony will take you into even greater trials.

Upon the eve of wedlock, you undergo opposition from others. Your previous confessors no longer understand you. You see your own humanity and experience aversion. Your fears intensify, telling you that you are following an imposter or that the True One will reject you after all. Suddenly you fall ill and the pain of it all is too much to bear.

But you are sent the mystical vision of a soft beckoning hand and you have a joy beyond comprehension. Somehow, any trial no longer matters. These truths allow you to open your throat for the wine to drain down the Grail stem into the holding tank of its foundational heart—the Seventh Dwelling Place.

The Seventh Dwelling Place

You meet Sophia face to face in the innermost chamber of intent. Her love is bottomless—no mock well here. Her vastness is such that your neurology cannot fathom meaning, but you are informed beyond the cellular level. You find this transmission as natural as the very blood circulating in the veins of existence. You are the drop absorbed in the ocean of timelessness. The marriage ceremony is complete and you must now return to your daily life, the container of the body and the limitations of the mind.

But your path is now simply more meaningful, your body is expanded and your mind is stretched. Exaltations are now a calm state of affairs. You bubble back up to the Grail bowl to be poured out and assimilated with expectancy.

Convergence

We won't find experience through the logical mind. We will find intellectual knowledge "about." In the First Dwelling Place, we are still so buffeted by our own internal dialogue; we only get momentary silences that alert us to some other possibility. By the time we enter the Second Dwelling Place, we have a genuine hunger that often becomes ravenous. And the bookshelves are filled to overflowing with all the knowledge we don't have. Many of us literally devour everything of any relevance we can grab, like so much bingeing through some fine gourmet buffet.

However, in the Fourth Dwelling Place, there are just a few books on a shelf and even fewer objects taking up space. This is because by the Third Dwelling Place, we've begun to have some direct experience; enough for us to discern what is real. In the Fourth Dwelling Place, it begins to become a way of life.

The more direct experience we've had, the less we need someone else to tell us how things are. We've become more and more apt to listen to the essence beyond tangibility. We've merged with it in such a way that we understand our own internal authority.

While I can't speak to others' process of immersion, I can relate what I witness of my own. There first comes an inner understanding of some core possibility of which I am very aware, but know little or nothing at all. My active embrace of the possibility creates a space, almost like a conduit. Being highly kinesthetic, I can only describe the feeling as an inner wavering. But it's not as though pulling away; it's more like a wave that I can't quite surf.

At that point, I usually begin to talk to others about whatever I am being schooled about in that moment. I do this even though I'm not yet able to consciously explain what I'm saying and even wonder why I'm saying it. The uncertainty comes because the logical mind hasn't yet caught the wave. However, there seems to be something about expression that creates arising bubbles of truth that engages the everyday part of me, thereby generating a relaxation into the wave. When that happens, the sea becomes calm. The integration takes place. The immersion is complete.

When we choose to engage with text and dialogue in the Fourth through Seventh Dwelling Places, it's the seed we use to grow our intelligence. Reading by then has become about spiritual practice, reinforcing alignment rather than filling the seams to bursting with things we thought we didn't know. In these Places, we recognize that we already know at a certain level. We don't even need to be reminded. The immersion remains steady.

So if you seek this place of no place—Teresa's *Seventh Dwelling Place*, the Tao Te Ching's *Absolute Reality*, the Jewish mystics' *Shekinah* and what I can only call *intent*, you will finally be struck by a transmission. You are struck first from within as you offer yourself to something not even consciously known.

The need to send out a signal comes from the existential angst of disconnection, disorientation or discomfort you suffer outside the castle walls. Thus, the offering goes out showing that you are readying yourself. And as you continue to hold yourself open, Sophia will come to permeate you. She will send to you what you ask in its purest sense, in the most perfect way, to exactly the places where you dwell, spurring you ever onward. You then cease to *do* so much as *be* and let your *being* shape your existence from within.

CHAPTER FOUR

Intentful Existence

My friend and I had been wandering through Korikancha, particularly lingering within what little was left of the Incan temple that had first resided there. After the conquistadors came to Peru, the sacred site was claimed by its conquerors, most of its initial structure demolished and a large Catholic church and monastery put in its place. Likely for political reasons, the Church chose to retain just a few small rooms from the original Incan Sun Temple. These rooms, dedicated to Illapa, the Storm God and hurler of lightning, were allowed to stand, now contained in the courtyard of the church complex. I had made my way completely around the courtyard when something across the way caught my eye.

The bulletin board on the wall just outside the tiny shop front had some very detailed information posted about preventing high-altitude sickness. Alongside was an article on Coca-Cola. I thought it mighty strange that a display partnered the story of the evolution of a commercial product with data on medical advice. Then I realized that the common denominator was the use of the coca leaf.

The sign over the door said *K'uychiwasi Qosqo*, Rainbow House of Cusco. Curious, I glanced inside the small space and was invited in by the brightly colored wares. Waving to my friend to let her know where I was going, I ventured inside.

A diminutive woman wearing clothing that seemed to swamp her small frame and a large brimmed black hat covered with folk art pins busied herself with something behind the counter. As I walked in, she glanced up, immediately broke into a big smile, her eyes, crinkling up behind wire-rimmed glasses, greeting me. I took a leisurely turn through the shop looking at cookies, candies, teas and artwork. By then, my friend had caught up with me and came in to investigate as well.

Seeing our apparent interest, Emma Cucchi Luini introduced herself and began to tell us of K'uychiwasi Qosqo's mission. The central purpose of this nonprofit organization was to educate about the uses of the coca leaf and its connection to the Andean culture. Actually, rather than connection, Emma emphasized that the coca leaf was the backbone of this ancient tradition, its practices and health of the native people.

Beleaguered with the discovery of a chemical extraction known as cocaine, the sacred coca leaf is now being threatened with extinction. Through tighter and tighter governmental controls and concurrent illicit operations, the simple coca farmer has been squeezed. Trying to scratch out a meager existence raising the same crops their ancestors have raised for centuries, these people are being directly affected by an encroaching Western culture in which a number of people substitute nose candy and greed for real experience.

In the last couple of decades, the national governments of Peru and Bolivia, pushed by the U.S. Drug Enforcement Agency, have targeted the coca leaf as the enemy, totally disregarding its cultural and quite innocent, but important, use by the indigenous peoples. The chewing of coca leaves is standard practice among the natives in the Andes, not to give them a high, but to increase their stamina for living and working in an environment that is often very difficult. Instead of inducing any undue alteration in their normal consciousness, which the coca leaf cannot relay at all in its natural form, its nutritional makeup provides them with energy and a plethora of nutrients not as available elsewhere in their sparse diet. Also ignored is its elevated status in the spiritual traditions and rituals of the Andean Indians. *Mama Coca* is the plant spirit invoked and Her leaves used in divinations, blessings and ceremonies. An analogy would be the chalice of wine symbolizing the blood of Christ in the communion ritual of many Christian religions.

As Emma so aptly put it, "There are many, many alcoholics in the world. Do they destroy the grape?"

That question certainly does make one think, particularly relative to what other motivations, political or otherwise, could possibly exist for the shortsighted methods used for eradicating cocaine trafficking through a focus on coca crops.

Could it be the genocide of indigenous peoples? That speculation may seem farfetched. However, look what the intentional slaughter of the buffalo did to the Plains Indians. Andean Indians little enjoy a similar status in their own countries as American Indians historically have in the United States.

Could it by any chance have to do with oil rich lands underlying the fields where coca is grown? Knowing what other convoluted methods of seizure and control have been used in the past, that may well explain some of the U.S. Government's extreme interest in the coca farmer.

The growers are caught in a web where, in order to feed their families, the choices currently available to them all seem so sticky that they cannot free themselves. The government will buy their crops for a pittance while the cocaine traffickers offer them six times that amount. The DEA will pay them to destroy their crops and say they will help the farmers to convert to another type of cultivation. However, the help promised never comes.

Enter Emma. With the in-country support of two Dominican friars, this Italian woman founded K'uychiwasi Qosqo in 1999.

Christo Deneumostier Grill, a young Peruvian man, has since joined her in her efforts. In addition to educating about the traditional and medicinal uses, they research new ways to use the coca leaf. In their quarters they help women, girls and young men in need by training them to produce cookies, candy and folk art using the coca leaf as an ingredient. They look forward to eventually create additional goods such as soaps.

In 2002, the organization even won the Slow Food Award for the Defense of Biodiversity, sponsored by the Slow Food Association originating in Italy. Emma and Christo are currently making small but painstaking steps within the bureaucracy of the Peruvian government toward wider distribution of their coca wares, the regulation of coca being tremendously tight. The only export of the leaf currently allowed is to the Coca-Cola Corporation in the United States. Ultimately, the success of Emma and Christo will benefit the Andean culture and help to maintain the growing of the coca leaf by offering products to be used by mainstream society.

As she finished her monologue, Emma shrugged and opened her hands in a characteristically Italian way and said, "I'm Italian. This cause doesn't even belong to me."

Reviewing our encounter in my mind later, I thought to myself, "This is a cause that belongs to the world. It belongs to us all. Emma chose to take it up."

To me, it doesn't matter where in the world the threads of ancient wisdom are being destroyed through thoughtless or misguided means. It's the concern of all individuals who understand the dangers of eradicating such traditions and the detrimental effect on the world's future, as we continue to lose sacred knowledge because of technological or political reasons, or just plain greediness.

Emma and I began to develop a friendship through sporadic e-mails after I returned to my home.

When I traveled again to Peru several months later, I visited her once more. This time I asked, "What is your story? How did you get here? How did you get involved in this work?"

My questions uncovered a fascinating tale and the meat of Emma's character emerged. I believe we can all learn a lot from this woman and others like her who hold unstinting intent and yet, humility.

She started the narrative at the beginning of her life by saying she was born near the Italian/Swiss border. Then she elaborated on her mother and father. She was very clear about giving credit to her parents for both their early and continued guidance and support.

"From my mother, I learned about culture and solidarity. Someone would knock on the door and my mother would say, 'What do you need?' And then she would give it to them, if she could. So, from her, I learned to be available to people.

"My father was a climber and he would take me with him. He would say, 'If you want to go with me, you walk. You are not here to be carried.' From him, I learned about nature and also discipline. He taught me that if there is a goal you have, you fix your sight on that goal and do what you need to do to move toward it. All these things, combined with my own energy and curiosity about the world, have served me well."

As a child, Emma was a focused student and seemed to know from an early time what she was about. She was eight years old when she began to say that she wanted to go where her hands were needed in the world. By the time she was fifteen years old, she had already discovered her lifelong hero and barometer to her own mission—Albert Schweitzer.

"He said that theoretical concepts are nothing unless you put them into action. Schweitzer opened his hospital in Africa under great difficulties. Even when his wife had to return to Switzerland for her health, he stayed on and continued his work. From him, I learned to put my ideals and mission before my personal needs and even my family.

"I knew that I always must move my mind and meet new challenges. I asked myself, 'Where is my root?' And I decided to enter medicine. But I would use medicine as an instrument, not as a goal."

In that conclusion, the spark of her dream toward being a humanitarian doctor caught fire.

As I listened to Emma, it seemed to me that the decision to use medicine as a tool rather than the end, along with her openness to continue to learn, was a decision paramount to her ability to move easily in the landscapes she traversed. She went on to medical school, and while she originally sought to be a surgeon, she finally decided to follow a specialty in anesthesiology because she could begin her practice much sooner. She wasn't viewed by fellow doctors and professors as one jockeying for position. Indeed, they knew that she would be gone as soon as possible in order to follow her work. Expressly because she was not considered a "threat," during her internship she was taken under the wing of various physicians and granted sundry opportunities to learn.

Her first break came in 1977 when she joined a climbing expedition to the mountain called Pucaranra in the Ancash region of Peru, as the team's doctor. Shortly after her return from this adventure she thought to move to Kenya to follow in the footsteps of her hero, Dr. Schweitzer. However, by that time, he had passed on. Due to his demise, the hospital he founded was in duress. His disciples were in a state of loss and confusion. The hospital was in chaos.

Not surprising, I thought to myself. What true teachings, or organizations, within the *spiritual* realm have been able to maintain the levels previously attained after their originators have transitioned? Mostly they become watered down and restrictive, the central wisdom forgotten or taken out of context. Why should a hospital formed by such a man not undergo similar disorientation?

Needing the structure no longer available at Dr. Schweitzer's hospital that she felt she required to learn tropical medicine, she opted for another location. She went to a hospital in northern Kenya, on the border of Ethiopia, where the people were enduring famine. There, after getting her feet wet, she began to work alongside and learn from the *bocor*, or tribal witch doctors. Emma respected the fact that many of their methods had healed people for centuries. Because the people saw that she respected their ways, she was also able to provide, in partnership with the witch doctors, those means from occidental medicine that filled a gap for such health threats as tetanus and meningitis.

After she had been there for a few years, she felt the need to move on in order to learn and contribute elsewhere. Emma saw an ad that had been placed in a professional journal by William and Gwen Mellon. These two extremely wealthy people had tired of the tidy life they were living in Arizona and wanted to give back what they could. In the midst of the dangerous upheaval of the presidency of Jean-Claude Duvalier, they sought to build a hospital in Haiti. In their ad, they were seeking volunteer doctors. Emma applied.

Standing in the airport, her family seeing her off to this unknown and rather risky venue after a visit home to Italy, her mother said to her, "Let me cry. You are going away now. You no longer belong to us. You belong to mankind."

Emma arrived in Haiti in 1981 at the age of 31 and stayed there for five years. In those perilous times and surrounded by the prevalent tribal religion Voodoo, she practiced the anesthesiology needed for surgeries. Not trusting the local electrical services to be stable, she chose to mix the old methods of her trade with the new.

"I would do the best I could according to what I was taught in school, but only within the means of the place. I would have the life of my patient by my hands. I didn't use the machines. The pulse is here," putting her fingers to her carotid artery. "I wanted to make sure they're alive. If the electricity went out, it would be disastrous."

She mentioned using a hand pump, sometimes for seven or eight hours, to continue ventilating during operations. In those years, she handled some 10,000 patients or more, only losing nine.

"I would hear the people buzzing out in the village when I walked by. Finally, I realized that they consider me a *bocor*! A witch doctor! From their eyes, in that room, we managed life! I put people to sleep and brought them out. The surgeon opens the body, takes the organs out, puts them back in and changes the life of the people."

Admittedly, working in the tribal culture where Voodoo, a powerful religion little understood by outsiders, was prevalent had its astounding and even, scary moments.

"One time we were invited to some celebrations. I was sitting on the outside of the circle when the people got up to dance. Someone invited me to join in. They use drums that create like a trance. The rhythm of the drums was getting louder and louder, and I was dancing. Then, I saw that all the women had moved away and it was only the men. They were dancing in a circle around me, getting closer and closer. For them, I was a different energy. And it was under the full moon, which was another symbol. I began to be afraid. There was no way out. I didn't know what to do. Suddenly, my colleague broke through the circle and snatched me out! I don't know what would have happened if he hadn't done that."

She talked about how the culture of Voodoo sometimes interfered with her work as an anesthesiologist.

"There was a young man who came to the clinic to have a cyst on his back removed. It only needed a local anesthetic, but the surgeon asked me if I would use a general on him because he was so scared of the surgery. So, I agreed.

She went on, "I administered the anesthetic and the surgeon asked me, 'Is he ready?' And I said, 'Yes. He is ready.' Just when she was ready to cut him with the knife, he broke all his restraints and sat straight up!

"We couldn't believe it! I gave him general anesthesia. It is not possible for any human to have the reflexes of the neck after administration of these drugs!"

The surgeon told everyone to stand back. "These are some energies stronger than us. Nobody move!" All watched, paralyzed, as the young man lurched to his feet and went home.

A few days later, the surgeon knocked on Emma's office door and indicated the same man had returned and wanted to talk to them. He said he knew that he had given them quite a shock. But, his *loá*, or spirit guide, didn't like the surgery. They were in conflict about it. He said he had now negotiated with his guide and wanted to go ahead with the surgery. He asked if they would still be willing to do it, which they were.

Emma smiled, "I made sure to use the same drug to show that my anesthesiology does work!"

From Haiti, Emma was invited to help open housing and a clinic for orphaned children in southern Sudan. The sponsors wanted a doctor who had wartime experience. With her tenure during the bloody downfall of the dictatorship of Duvalier, she fit the bill.

One of the boys there had an infection in his leg that had turned gangrenous. Given the limited capabilities of the clinic, the doctors didn't hold out much hope for him. Knowing that there were means to save him in Italy, Emma raised the money through different organizations and made arrangements to send the boy to her homeland for the needed treatment. She accompanied him. There, the doctors were able to save not only his life, but almost his entire foot. He ended up losing only a couple of toes. He stayed in Italy to recuperate, was eventually adopted and has now applied for medical school and intends to return to his original home to help his people.

On her way back to Sudan, Emma laid over in Khartoum. She was told that the only air transportation going to her village, a military plane, had been shot down. For three days she awaited conveyance. On the evening of the third day she was having dinner with other foreign travelers in a hotel restaurant when terrorists bombed this establishment frequented by Westerners. Twenty-nine people lost their lives. Emma was the only survivor. She was also the only doctor available because entry to the area was barred after the attack. That same night the U.S. Embassy and a U.S. club in Khartoum were also bombed.

With one eardrum blown and her other ear injured, she had otherwise miraculously escaped serious physical injury. Without any real equipment, she did the best she could for people. And what she finally could do was only to help the injured die.

Airlifted out, she flew home to Italy to heal. But it was more than her physical body that needed healing. Her spirit was devastated. Emma had lost the meaning of the path to which she had given her life. How could she continue when culture and religion separate people in such horrible ways?

After eight months in Italy her parents said to her, "This is your house, but you know you cannot stay here."

When an Italian association contacted her about an assignment in Bolivia, she half-heartedly accepted. But she stayed to herself and didn't connect with the people.

"These Quechua people were so quiet, so shy. I was used to Africa with the dancing, the celebration! I didn't like it there. Coca? What's coca? I didn't get involved."

After two years the International Red Cross tendered her an offer at their hospital in war-torn Somalia. She snapped it up. There she remained for another two years. Then, she was asked to return to Bolivia by the Italian association that had previously sponsored her.

However, by that time, Emma had made the decision that she no longer wanted to work with associations. Her intent was to found her own humanitarian organization, to include a clinic and other needed services.

"I will find my own place like Dr. Schweitzer and stop," she decided.

She was referring to the fact that Schweitzer founded his hospital in Gabon and remained there, dedicated to his work, until his death another 53 years later. But at the time, she hadn't yet found her place.

The Italian association begged her, saying they needed just six more months from her in Bolivia. She protested. They enticed her. It would be just like what Schweitzer had done. This time, instead of the highlands, they said, it will be the jungle where you will work on a project to see about medical needs.

The enticement worked. Emma departed for Bolivia. There the association gave her a Toyota Land Cruiser and told her that if, in her duties, she was near the Catholic mission, she was welcome to sleep there. Otherwise, she would have to sleep in the car.

Emma didn't know it at the time, but realized later, "They threw me alone into the middle of the narcotic trafficking area! The missionaries were leaving! They said, 'It's too dangerous for us. But you're young. You have much enthusiasm!'"

Coming from her own sense of utter dedication no matter what, she was thrown into religious conflict. She saw the Church putting a priority of the missionaries' safety over the needs of the people they were to serve. Making a clear distinction between religion and spirituality, Emma found that the actions of the Church didn't deter her spirituality or her mission to help others.

In the midst of the active presences of narcotic traffickers, the Bolivian army and police and the U.S. DEA, she began to explore the villages on the borders of the jungle to see where she could assist them. There she met the coca growers.

They said, "You must visit us where we live."

Emma came back with, "This is the end of the world! Beyond there is just jungle!"

They assured her, "Farther than the monkeys and the snakes, we live. And here we have our crops of coca."

Venturing into those thick, humid places was, for Emma, like Dr. Schweitzer arriving in Africa in 1913. They moved through the density via canoes and cut swathes in the compact vegetation with machetes. There was no running water or electricity in the villages, but plenty of jaguars surrounding them. The farmers told her they needed her help.

Emma decided she had found her place.

She had been writing a book, *Walk in the Sun*. She told them, "If I can get my book published and get some money from that, I will come back and help you."

With the help of family and friends she was able to get her book published in Italy. Miraculously, it seemed, within three months' time she had collected $30,000 through book sales by promoting it in groups and colleges. She let potential readers know that she was raising funds to build a small medical clinic in the jungles of Bolivia for people in much need of aid.

Emma returned to the jungle and began to build her clinic. She continued going from village to village supporting the women and attending the people's medical needs.

She noticed that when she would visit them in their homes or where they gathered, they would often have a pile of coca leaves in a conspicuous place. The Indians continually kept a little wad in their cheeks, their saliva drawing out the juice, which they then swallowed. Emma noticed that they would perform a ritual before inserting the leaves. The chewing of coca leaves seemed to be a communal practice.

Emma was curious, but held back. "That would be like me going into someone's house and helping myself to a cup of coffee. So, I waited."

One day her waiting was over. As she was sitting with the villagers one day, one of them said, "You want *chajchado*?" He gestured toward the pile of coca leaves on the table, inviting her to partake of the ritual practice.

From that point, Emma knew she was accepted into the community. She started chewing coca like a native, and began to notice its effects on her ability to sustain energy for long durations. Using her scientific background, she conducted simple experiments on herself relative to its nutritional benefits. She found that when she didn't practice *chajchado* she would tire more easily and require food more frequently. Indeed, some years later through clinical research undertaken by a Peruvian scientist, she was able to validate the enormous amount of nutrients in that simple plant.

But even back then, she began to have a firm conviction related to the paramount importance of the coca leaf to the Indians' health as well as spiritual tradition. Referring to the factions surrounding them, she told the growers, "If they destroy coca, they will destroy *you* because of the petrol underground. You will become militarized!"

With this statement, Emma made the unwitting foray into the political aspects of this natural substance. When the Bolivian police and U.S. DEA agents came through the growers' villages, they would demand, "Who is this woman? She is a *gringa*?"

The villagers would tell them, "No, she is not a *gringa*. She is our *campaniera*, our friend." The Indians protected her, but some of them were bribed.

Emma felt the undercurrents that told her something was wrong. It became a common occurrence that when she would pass through the checkpoint, returning from the jungle, sometimes very late at night, the police would harass her. They would try to provoke a conflict with her. Sometimes they succeeded.

In early August 1994, she returned to a village where she sometimes stayed briefly to obtain supplies before returning to the jungle. She was awakened early in the morning by a sharp knock on the door of her hut. Emma opened the door to an army of twenty policemen and agents!

"Are you Emma Cucchi?"

"Yes."

"You are accused of terrorism. Come with us."

Shocked, Emma complied and was taken to a compound where her jailers kept her overnight. There she endured an all night beating with sticks. She was thrown repeatedly on the floor. The following day she was taken to the political police in La Paz where she was kept for three days. There she was accused of all manner of terrorist acts. She was told she supplied $50,000 worth of arms to the coca growers in order for them to rise up against the Bolivian government. She was charged with being part of a terrorist group.

Ultimately, she was found to be interfering with Bolivia's political issues and deported to Italy where her passport was revoked. She was entered into immigration databases as a *persona non grata* and is still barred to this day from entering Bolivia and the United States.

There was no proof of any of the accusations, but her enemies had done a good job of perpetuating the falsehoods. Reporters grabbed hold of the news and the story of the "Italian terrorist doctor" and Emma's face was widely splashed and trashed across journalistic media.

When she spoke of the effects, she did so with great sadness and hurt, "It caused such problems for my family, even now after all these years. People turn away on the street."

Perhaps even most appalling and disheartening is the fact that the associations, for whom Emma had selflessly worked so diligently, disappeared. These were people who certainly should have known better given her long record of dedication. But they wanted nothing to do with her or the publicity.

There was only one public figure who sustained her—the Archbishop of Milan. He commiserated with her and encouraged her. He claimed, in essence, that she must return to the fire. If she were no longer able to go to Bolivia, then she would gain ground somewhere else.

The Archbishop knew of a couple of Spanish Dominican friars who were working with coca growers in Peru. After allowing Emma some time to get over her shellshock, he communicated with the friars and said, "Take her." The friars, in turn, contacted Emma and worked the bureaucratic system to obtain the permits needed for her to join them and continue her work in some way. She arrived in Peru in October 1995. By January 1999, she had found solid footing and, with the support of the friars, created the foundation now called *K'uychiwasi Qosqo.*

Emma smiled, "This is the only place I haven't chosen myself."

She paused seeming to reflect for a moment and continued, "And this is the place I am doing more. Sometimes you get your life together, not where you want to, but where you *must* go. The energy of life goes toward the place it must go."

She took a deep breath and exhaled, "Sometimes you resist. Sometimes I want to be in Bolivia, not in Peru. But I have to ask why I wasn't killed there."

There's an obvious answer—pure intent and the Divinity that protects those who hold it. Emma's fuller work is now just evolving.

The Relentless Path

In the typical sense, Emma's path is not for everyone. But in another sense, perhaps it is. She followed her pure intent of service to others. In doing so, she had experiences that were extraordinary in their joy and their pain. She also had the more usual and mundane times we all pass in living from one day to the next. All of these occurrences took her on a venture inward to discover her Core Self. That is one way for intent to manifest its wider nature.

Another way is to start with the cleaning of the self. By focusing on cleansing away any caking or spattering of mud that may seek to obliterate that Core Self, the intent of an authentic life can also be manifested. Just so, it can take us from a focus toward Core Self that then can emanate real consciousness to others.

We were making our way slowly along the narrow shelf that passed for a trail on the mountainside where the Pisaq ruins were located. It was the group's fourth day in Peru. I was near the front, following closely behind Don Américo.

Before he even turned around to see with his normal vision, he called out a warning in Spanish to his son Gáyle, who was bringing up the rear, "The white one has an attraction for the abyss!"

At that point, I swiveled around. My eyes swept the staggered line of individuals I had brought down to Peru to experience Andean mysticism, the land and Her people. My gaze stopped in amazement on Audrey, identified in Don Américo's call to Gáyle by her completely white hair. Here was a woman with whom I had engaged on a continual basis in the last year. She was one who, through unrelenting commitment, had undergone incredible shifts of consciousness in a very short time. Based upon the overwhelming courage she exhibited of facing whatever emerged in our work together, the woman I now saw was unknown to me.

Even from my viewpoint, I could discern her quaking fear. She was the last in line, except for Gáyle who seemed to be guarding her. Almost hugging the mountainside, she crab walked, inches at a time, her body rigid, her face agitated.

As it turned out, Audrey had a phobia of heights. Had she mentioned this fact to me over the past year, we could have released it easily. But, she later told me, she thought the issue irrelevant. I know the effect that phobias can have since I had one of heights earlier in my own life. I recalled the paralyzing state of affairs I used to endure on the rare occasion I was in a high place free of solid walls. Remembering the way my knees used to turn watery while waves of anxiety rushed through me, my heart went out to her.

If a fear of this nature were going to emerge in anyone, Pisaq would be a place for it to do so. The trail started out much wider and it's easy enough to be distracted from its narrowing by the fascinating beauty of this sacred place, or the sweet little native girls posing for photos with their lambs. Suddenly rounding a bend, for a long stretch the path ranged solely about two to three feet wide, and the altitude and great drop were apparent. I know it had my attention. On the other hand, the children, who were well used to the conditions, played and ran along like young mountain goats in their flimsy sandals or bare feet.

Knowing that she was in Gáyle's excellent hands and also seeing the person in front of her stopping to hold out a hand for Audrey to grasp for security, I turned around and continued to follow Don Américo's lead. Periodically we stopped and waited until all caught up.

Once Don Américo directed us to climb up a large rock outcropping on the outer side of the trail. Being first up, I looked at him in askance. There seemed to be no apparent footing to follow or easy way to hoist myself up. I couldn't see any real reason at the time to take this little detour either. He merely continued to urge me on with his gesture. So I complied, finally finding my way up a ledge and around to the top. The others followed, Audrey included, albeit slowly and taking hands proffered in help. When everyone was settled, we did a short meditation. In that time, a group of tourists passed on the trail below us. Presently, Don Américo indicated that we should return to the trail.

The trip off the outcropping was perhaps even more interesting than the climb up. As sometimes happens, the descent looked much steeper than the ascent to get there. After I was on even ground myself, I watched for Audrey. She came into my view after rounding a large rock, talking to herself the whole way.

"Let's see. This foot goes here. And now this foot goes there. There we go! OK. Put that hand there. Now what? Yes. Let me sit down and I can slide from here. No, it's OK. I can do this."

And she plopped down to stand with those of us waiting, receiving cheers of encouragement and pats on the back. Whether Don Américo really had us take that side trip to avoid tourists or to push us all some more, I don't know. He is often prone to the latter. I do know that I now saw quite an adjustment in Audrey's demeanor. Her countenance had a sense of fearlessness to it, her stature straighter and taller.

As we all congratulated her, she said, "What else was I going to do? I certainly wasn't going to turn around. All I *could* do was go forward! And everyone was so supportive."

Don Américo proclaimed her a warrior of the spirit and we continued on our walking journey around Pisaq. By the time we had returned to where we left our driver, and during the rest of our time in Peru together, Audrey accepted helping hands periodically just as the others sometimes did. But mostly she traversed wide and narrow paths on her own, even finding the ability to look out over the valleys of high places.

Much later as I was considering stories to include in this particular chapter, I asked her permission to write of her radical revolution from panic to tranquility. Outside the therapeutic environment, it's a rare occurrence for me to witness someone undergo such a transformation in a matter of a couple of hours. To me, the basis came from strong intent, actually not unlike what she had exhibited during our previous work together.

"Did it really seem that profound?" she asked me.

After I assured her that it did, she elaborated, "It certainly did on the inside. And it's still with me. As I'm going out in the world, they expect certain things of me." Audrey had recently taken a job after being retired for some time. "I just say to myself, put one foot in front of the other. That's what I can do."

One of the great validations she brought up repeatedly when talking about her experience was the real understanding about being in the present moment, and how fear was mostly an anticipation of something that hadn't and likely wouldn't happen.

"I said to myself, 'I'm here right now. Putting this foot here. Now, what is it everyone is looking at? Oh! The beauty of the valley is incredible!' Worrying about falling, I had missed a lot of that."

That's exactly right. Worry paralyzes the body and the mind, taking us out of the real experience to be had. If we succumb to worry, we project a future that doesn't even exist. These were real words of wisdom from a woman who assuredly realized the power that intent has to move us beyond obstacles into living an unencumbered life.

Things happened perfectly. If Audrey and I had collaborated in my office to release her phobia, not only would we all have lost the opportunity to witness such a spectacular example of self-healing, but Audrey herself would have been deprived of the dramatic confirmation of her own abilities. Equally important to her was the group support.

"I know I'm not alone," she said some time later as she reflected back on our collective time. "We all had things to deal with, but we gave loving support to each other."

We aren't alone. Intent is there. If we carry that, natural Divine forces will provide to us what upholds it.

Audrey added one last thought, "I was continually buying all these self-help books. I guess I was looking for the magic sentence that was going to do it all for me rather than doing my own work. What I realize is that is the author's experience, but not mine. I'm going to take all those self-help books down to the used bookstore!"

The Ambient Effect

We are born with intent. We all have our own relationships and discoveries related to it based on what we are to learn. One way is not better than another way. The activation of intent in our lives is perfect for our own deeper purposes of awakening.

Some people, like Emma, know from early on what fuels their inner soul and move with undeniable faith toward what will fulfill it. Others of us have sporadic glimpses, but may be focused on too small a vessel, already overfilled, to recognize the signals. This would be analogous to the Zen master pouring tea for his disciple. The master pours and pours until tea is running over the brim of the cup and onto the floor. When the disciple protests, the master says, "I cannot tell you anything. Your cup is already too full." So it is for many of us and we bloom later, when we have finally heard the master called Intent and empty our cups.

Living through intent doesn't mean it's necessarily a smooth road. Part of intent is moving through any intention that exists. Mostly it's about adhering to a process that teaches us to walk upright. First we're lying on our backs waving our feet in the air. Then, something calls us to turn over and scoot or crawl. We eventually put our hands on a support and pull ourselves up. Finally, we make those faltering and then smoother steps on our own. Ultimately, we find we can climb mountains.

It doesn't mean we don't have doubts or fears. Emma and Audrey are the people they are expressly because they've engaged the inner courage and love to meet and move through any disillusionment, doubt or regret. People who are clear at a certain level—even if what is swirling around them is unclear, unseen or illusional—have the ability to see through the mist to the point where the direction becomes apparent.

During a later leg of the same Peru journey with Audrey, I was walking once again immediately behind Don Américo on a high trail. Dusk was quickly fading and night was near. We had been meditating further up the mountain and were now headed back to our quarters. We were strung for some distance along the uneven, rocky path, little groupings or an individual here and there. I was watching the ground in front of me so as not to slip and fall. I glanced up and saw the back of Don Américo a few feet in front of me as he continued his lead.

Suddenly, I had the most bizarre, unnerving experience. I saw his eyes gazing at me through the back of his head! Thinking I was crazy, I quickly looked down at the ground again and then stole another look. His gaze was still there! I willed my eyes to remain in that position. I had some sense of an image of his full face emerging as well, as his attention moved beyond me and swept the rest of the group. When I told him of my observation later, he just giggled and elaborated no further.

When intent is resolute, it engenders a certain kind of awareness beyond the five senses. It directs a consciousness that allows all-pervading vision, touch without presence, smell of the beyond and sound of creation. Thus, undeniable guidance is always given.

The Tasking

Set your intent and let it go. Your intent is your beginning. Worrying about the details detracts from the intent. In your strong intent, the attraction will take care of the details.

The first aspect of beginning is assessing yourself and taking responsibility for your own course, where it has taken you and where you are now. That responsibility will determine your future—the one that exists through the vibration you now exude.

This is the Separation and then the Search. It isn't really a search as much as it is a surrendering to intent. The giving over is to intent. Then intent takes the lead and brings you what will take you further. It will take you further to recognize your Core Self, the Self that had been hidden from you previously, but the one that had been there all along.

Sometimes the realization comes through sitting still—through patience and listening. It's *not* listening to what has been habit, but listening to the quieter place and the guidance there.

Sometimes the realization comes through an action, but only an action made from clarity, from impeccability. Otherwise, it's an action taken from habit. Then the action will merely tell you something about your habit.

An action arising from the deeper place will have a solid knowing and urging about it. It's a bodily felt energy that envelops you in knowing. It's not a feeling of desperation accompanied by inappropriate or castigating internal voices. That's the dialogue through which the actions of habit are fulfilled.

Actions of impeccability move you along the warrior's path of utter surrender to the destiny of knowing and not knowing. It is the knowing of the Core Self in all aspects, in all human tendencies, in all that is resident of Source. It is the not knowing of the profound comfort of the Infinite.

It is the mind overtaken by Spirit.

It is the mind having willingly succumbed to the wider wisdom dwelling within and without.

And you have to leave the place of previous comfort and familiarity in order to uncover it.

CHAPTER FIVE

Connecting with the Cosmos

I sat waiting silently, idly gazing around the room, taking in my surroundings for the umpteenth time. I wanted to carefully preserve my memory of this place that had come to mean so much to me. I filed away the rough, wide-planked floor of the old hacienda where so many feet had walked over the centuries. Those feet had belonged to spiritual and political leaders, parents seeking baptism of their new-born babies, villagers asking for counsel, visitors like myself from various countries looking for renewal, as well as the domain's many generations of inhabitants. I smiled to myself as I once again noted the large bowing in the middle of the ceiling, looking for all the world as though it would release its pregnant load at any moment. Listening to the bees buzzing loudly right outside the wide windows that bathed the room in late afternoon light, I wondered if the home they had made in the walls years ago had anything to do with the ceiling's womb-like appearance. I made a picture in my mind of the weight becoming too much one day soon and golden honey pouring through the cracks to cover the long wooden dining table directly underneath with a sticky treasure.

But my friend and I were safe from an opening of that nature, if not from others. We were sitting at the far end of the long room in a square of padded wooden benches and chairs, a llama skin rug underneath our feet. I glanced over at her. She didn't look at all worried. She wore the same defocused look I probably had.

I returned to loading my memory bank. Through the windows, I could see the grassy clearing that I knew led to the wildish garden containing surprising rooms made from fallen trees and overgrown vines, the perfect spots to hide away for contemplation. Steeply terraced peaks comprised the backdrop that framed this scene. The ground dropped drastically to a river far below. It was called the highlands of Peru for a reason.

The door to the outside opened. We both looked up in anticipation. A young Indian girl of about fourteen entered the room carrying a pan that smoked profusely. She had the most serious face I have ever seen on a child. It wasn't a face of disapproval, pain or fear. It was the face of someone who saw things others didn't see, and perhaps didn't yet know how to reconcile that fact with what she might otherwise have been taught.

She looked askance at the man who was seated with us, the owner of the house. Don Américo made a gesture and the girl proceeded to walk around the room. When she got closer my nose picked up the pungent smell of the aromatic wood smoldering on the hot coals. She walked up to each of us, waited for us to bathe ourselves in the smoke and then continued on into each room. Likely having decided that the house was now clear, she walked back to the door and withdrew. I sat, already in a trancelike state, the smell of the incense having put me in a timeless place.

In a short time, the girl re-entered, still with the pan of coals, but without the smoking contents. A woman perhaps in her early thirties accompanied her. Doña Flora held one layer of her multi-tiered skirts in such a way as to make a basket for its load of plant matter. On her head she wore the traditional dish-shaped, brightly colored hat, with a woven chinstrap keeping it in its place. Doña Flora made her way over, dipping her head slightly to each of us, saying something softly in Quechua. Her daughter Yasmin followed closely behind.

The two of them busied themselves quietly in the space between us on the floor. Yasmin began stripping the leaves from their stalks. When she had a handful, she handed them to her mother, who held the bundle over the hot coals. In a few minutes she turned them to their other side, the heat warming and wilting them. After the herb began emitting its comforting sweetish scent, Doña Flora rose with bundle in hand and moved over to my friend who sat with her eyes closed. Starting at the top of her head, she wiped her down with the limp leaves, all the while speaking almost inaudibly what I assumed was a blessing. When she determined the plants held all they could, Yasmin was ready with more. Doña Flora continued the cleaning until she had covered the entire body, down to stocking feet.

As I was aware of Doña Flora preparing the plants for me, I closed my eyes in readiness and sat forward in my seat. Her hands pressed the warm leaves onto the top of my head, holding them there. I could feel her gentle breath expelling itself between words onto my hair as she leaned in close, urging the blessing into my crown. I could feel something inside me respond, taking hold. Although she swabbed my clothed body, something else happened beyond the physical that I couldn't describe to myself. Not wanting to manipulate its meaning, I just surrendered to the experience. After Doña Flora was through with me, I could hear her moving on to Don Américo. I pushed myself back onto the bench to find the support of its back and remained with my eyes closed. I stayed that way for some indeterminate time, not willing to give up the comforting cocoon in which I dwelt. There I allowed myself to remain, experiencing a continued lightness and warmth. When I finally opened my eyes, it was because I'd heard the sounds of Doña Flora and Yasmin gathering the implements of the cleaning ritual, preparing to leave us.

"Gracias, Mama," Doña Flora and I said to each other, holding each other's shoulders and bringing our cheeks to touch. "Gracias," the word having a soft dipping and shushing sound in the middle rather than the typical harder Spanish pronunciation.

I felt such a profound esteem for this sweet native woman with the wide, open face and shy, unassuming manner. With such a humble demeanor, I wondered if she had any realization of how powerful she was. Perhaps a discernible lack of ego was one aspect that made her even more effective, her healing abilities coming from an inner place of reverence.

My mind glanced over a story Don Américo had relayed to me some time earlier.

"Flora is a *paco*," he said. He talked about the distinction of the Quechua word *paco*, meaning a person with special gifts who particularly worked with plants, invoking energy through ceremony in order to heal. In recent years in our culture, we've come to call someone like this a shaman, although I doubt many understand the true meaning of this designation.

He went on to say how, some years earlier, Doña Flora either didn't know about or didn't accept her abilities. She became extremely ill. This sickness continued to worsen. It seemed no one could do anything to help her. The medical doctors were also unable to diagnose anything.

During one of his visits to Salk'a Wasi, his ancestral home, located adjacent to the Mollamarka Indian village, Don Américo went to see her. As she lie prone, he began to work on her with *q'uyas*, or stones, used for healing and connecting. He labored over her, touching the stones to her physical body and moving through her energy field, wiping away what could have caused her illness. Suddenly a light formed between the stone and her body. The light grew in size and brightness until it became a large ball that moved down her body and then—disappeared. She immediately began to recover. It was after this experience and a return to health that she began to work with plants and undertook her healing work with intent.

I reflected on her story as I trod up the mountain after our afternoon sojourn. At the hour of power—that magic point between daytime and nighttime—Don Américo, his protégé, my friend and I were walking to a high point to witness the sun slip to its rest. As I sat there, I realized that something was different. I couldn't discern specifically what that difference was, or put it into words. But I knew without a doubt that something in me had shifted to a better place. I carried that certainty with me back down the mountain and to my bed later that night.

The next day Doña Flora and Yasmin returned about the same time. As before, we waited for them in the same place, with anticipation, for the completion of their work with us. First, it had been necessary to clear from us what debris we inadvertently carried with us to that place from the ordinary world. Being as pristine in that realm as possible, we were then prepared for the next aspect, a push to the *left side*. The left side is the place of connection, the realm of the Mystery, the feminine aspect of receptivity. From that side comes the experience of insight—not the mental noting of it— that can flood the right-sided life with richness previously not lived.

Again, Yasmin cleared the house with her smoking pan. Meanwhile, her mother deposited on the floor a ball of yarn and a few stalks of the same herb used the previous day. When her daughter had exited the room and returned, the *paco* Doña Flora arranged the plants in a star shape on the floor. When she was satisfied with the arrangement, she stood. Inviting my friend to remove her shoes and socks, she motioned for her to come stand on top of the plants. Then, taking the yarn in her hand, Doña Flora put one end under the big toe of my friend's foot. She began winding it around her body, until she encased her to the top of her head in a string shrouding that passed around her joints and major energy centers of the body. No sooner did Doña Flora complete the wrapping than she immediately begin to undo it, snapping the yarn and breaking it quickly with her hands at each juncture of the body that she deemed necessary. All the while, she spoke softly and rapidly in Quechua, compelling the string to do its work as she stored the broken pieces in her other hand. After all string had been removed, Doña Flora used the yarn bundle to wipe my friend down from head to foot, much as she had the day before with the leaves. When done, she handed the yarn laden with heavy energy to Yasmin, who was crouched on the floor to one side. Yasmin hid the bundle in her skirts to contain it. My friend stepped back to her seat, her body relaxed.

Doña Flora turned to me expectantly. I arose and moved to the ritual space. I felt the leaves cool underneath my bare feet, sticking to them as I shifted to find my balance. Closing my eyes, I perceived the narrow pressure of the yarn being wound around my big toe and continuing in intervals up my body, joining my legs together, pinning my arms to my sides, slightly cutting into the base of my throat and sealing my eyes shut. I was aware of a sense of feeling tied and cut off, something that was not unfamiliar to me in the past if I allowed myself to become unconsciously encased in the right-sided world. Immediately following that fleeting awareness, I began to experience both a literal and a metaphorical loosening and lessening. Hearing the snapping, the breaking of my ties and Doña Flora's voice compelling something to let go, to shift, generated what I can only describe as an effervescent quality in the interior of my body that surrounded me as well. It was as though something was opened inside that was flowing outward in gentle waves. I knew from past experience this sensation to be an expansion of my subtle energy field. But it was different somehow.

The brushing of the wool over my head and face signaled to me that Doña Flora was collecting any remnants of heaviness that may have remained in my field. When I felt the yarn softly scratching my feet, I knew she was done. I opened my eyes and sensed rather than saw her deliver the soiled package to Yasmin, who immediately departed from the room, the *hucha*, or heavy energy, safely restrained in her closely held skirts. Doña Flora gathered her simple instruments, dipped her head to us, and soon left as well.

Seated once again, I began to detach myself from my surroundings. But before I completely moved into a meditative state, I heard Don Américo remark that a man was waiting to run swiftly all the way down to the river to deposit the *hucha*. The river would cleanse the heaviness, eventually carrying anything remaining to the sea where it would be dispersed.

A few hours later when we made our daily journey up the mountain to witness the transition of the day, I remarked to my friend that I felt like I had just emerged squeaky clean from a long, hot shower.

The sun had already set behind the mountain, but it wasn't yet dark. It truly seemed like the point between two worlds at that moment. The four of us had paired off and were performing *Yanachacuy*, a process of giving and receiving energy. I was standing back to back with Don Américo, the whole length of our bodies touching, as we passed the energy of what each needed between us. I began to feel a mounting pressure in the top of my head that escalated, but not to the point of discomfort. When we separated I was experiencing a buzzing in my body that was familiar to me.

But no sooner had I moved over to his protégé and our spines touched, than I felt what I could only characterize as a solid column of uncontrollable energy descending through my crown that did not stop. Some potent force was surging into a vessel that felt too small to contain it all. Sudden nausea made me know that I was going to toss my cookies if I didn't break contact with my partner. I quickly moved away and stood still for a moment to get my bearings, and the nausea lessened. The others looked questioningly at me, but I said nothing.

Don Américo urged us into a circle to further enhance the energy. We joined hands and I gazed over his shoulder at the mountain across the ravine directly in my line of sight. While I have had a number of what some people may view as unusual experiences, up until that time I had never experienced the exponential force and raw power of what happened next.

As I continued to look at the line where the mountain and sky met, a brilliant light flashed from the highest peak. It locked onto my eyes. As though a laser was piercing me and would not let me go, the light got brighter and brighter until it filled my whole head. It filled my whole being. I began to lose the edges of my body and dissipate. I was merging into some vastness that had no form, only light.

With what semblance of the material plane I had left, I broke with the circle and barely stumbled over to a rock where I quickly sat down. I closed my eyes to try to shake what was happening, it seeming again to be too much for me. When I opened them, I saw lightning coming *from* the mountaintop. Breathless, I turned my head to look at the other mountains around me. Wherever I looked, lightning emerged all along the ridges striking into the sky. This resplendent scene continued for several minutes until it began to fade from my eyes. Finally, only the subtle energy field of the mountains was left to my vision.

I continued to sit on the stone where I had sought grounding until the earth felt firmer beneath my feet. About that time, Don Américo and his protégé rounded the path. Aware that something had been happening, he had knowingly given me the space for it to unfold and was now back to collect me. My friend was doing her own meditation about fifty feet away. He motioned to us and we all picked our way down the darkening trail.

The ground beneath me once again felt solid and I could distinguish my body from its surrounding environment. Yet, something had happened for which my logical mind had no answer. How does someone explain having received a transmission from a mountain?

Or perhaps from the Cosmos? If there is an explanation, perhaps it's that after the clearing ritual Doña Flora performed and the subsequent *Lloq'enecuy* ceremony, the push to the *left side*, my frequency more cleanly and similarly resonated with cosmic energies, the ones that birth us all. Whether this is an accurate summation or not, I can only sense my own truth therein. However, I do know the effect that I believe came from it.

Shortly thereafter, I went back to my home from Peru. Upon my return, I became aware that I somehow knew things I hadn't known in quite the same way before. These were such things about the nature of existence and the ways of the Universe. A deep trust followed that knowing that has led me into increasing clarity and insight into my own life, as well as it having spilled over into my work with others. I am also certain, without a doubt, that this connection is available to everyone who chooses it.

Clearing

Part of choosing this connection is to make a space for it to pass through. The Cosmos and all its subtleties are always present. For most of us, though, it runs in the background like music we barely attune to as we're doggedly fixated on some chore. When taken as backdrop noise its presence is overlooked. Or, only when our underlying intent becomes overwhelming does it find the slit to slide into awareness. Even so, this correspondence is often passed off as imagination or coincidence or otherwise rationalized. The communication is forever transmitted, but it takes a conscious receiver to catch it.

We are taught to compartmentalize our lives into work, play, family, spiritual, creative time and so on, through the dogma of a materialistic culture and time management gurus so that everything will get done! We have busy lives and the goal is to be balanced and have everything in its appropriate slot!

Since this is the current reality most people are dealing with, so be it. Until we truly realize that all life is meant to be integrated and that compartmentalizing existence is artificial, we will tap into very little except the sharp corners of a life rendered so. Indeed, it is the segmenting, the stop/start, that interrupts a flow.

However, we must all start where we are. Making the literal and metaphoric space—regular time and place—is a necessary step until cosmic connection becomes naturally interwoven in our lives. Making a compartment for it to happen is probably the first aspect of having it for most of us. Merely wishing for a depth of experience generally won't put it there. Something must signal that intent.

By choosing to engage in a clearing practice at a regular interval and in a particular place, you can create an opening. When you return there again and again with intent, you generate a vibration that begins to resonate outside the ordinary world. Just going through the motions mechanically won't do it. But giving a practice ritual attention will intensify its power. This kind of focus to meaning and desire enfolds something. It catches us up in a further realm of reality, one that is operating right within the everyday one but generally goes unnoticed.

In order to tap into this aspect of existence, we must shed what would obliterate that opportunity. All of us have things resident within us, like so many parasites living from the life force we generate. If we are unaware of this condition, we perpetuate whatever we have picked up along the way. We invite a feeding frenzy that expands itself, until we finally wake up and wonder why we're feeling so drained or can't get where we want to go.

It's necessary to release any limiting life beliefs that generate the thought forms that keep us stuck. Additionally, if we don't know the boundaries of the self, where we leave off and others start, it's all too easy to merge and engage others' energies as our own or allow our life force to be inadvertently siphoned off. Finally, we can pick up toxicities from environments where we engage, if our fields are permeable in that way, unless we are alert to that possibility.

Energy is related to lightness and heaviness rather than a judgment of goodness or badness. There is a felt sense. We can literally feel if it bolsters us up or weighs us down. If we are able to maintain lightness in our energy field, then we can surf the wave. When we become heavy, it's much easier to get sucked in by the undertow that may be present in pockets of life.

A practice is a ritual that allows a cleaning to take place. However, the clearing doesn't follow if we only go through the motions. Then, it merely becomes like the genuflection that we may perform because we were taught to do so when young and the family around us frowned if we didn't. The level of understanding isn't there. Without intent, nothing happens. In that case, a practice becomes just another rule to follow in a long string of shoulds.

This failure would become one more thing for which we could say to ourselves, "I'm doing what I'm supposed to do, what the books say to do, what the teachers teach. Why isn't it happening for me?" A detour from the course happens when people mistake a practice or ceremony for the end. The truth is that it's a means. The end is the opening and what lies beyond. The end is generated from intent to engage with our true natures. And thus, the end is That.

CHAPTER SIX

What Matters

When I was seven years old, my parents and I lived in condemned military housing across the river from Washington D.C. for a short year. The place where we lived later turned into one of the Arlington Cemetery parking lots. My father was attending French language school before we were sent to Paris for nearly five years.

On either side of the boulevard leading to the cemetery were wide strips of green, sparsely furnished with trees. My mother and I used to take walks through this area on our way to the Potomac, Georgetown or any number of places. The squirrels playing in what trees there were fascinated me.

Those bands of land and its inhabitants garnered my attention to such a degree that when given the assignment that year to pen a short story for school, I wrote about it. *The Empty Treed Forest* formed itself out of the idealism of my very young mind and told the plight of the animals whose homes had been stripped from them. This tale was in the far recesses of my mind until the past year when an event brought it back with an even fuller personal and global meaning.

I was bathing in the rosy afterglow from a retreat completed the day before, puttering around my downtown office, when I was slammed into re-entering everyday reality. I received an excited phone call from a longtime participant of my workshops. She alerted me to the wildly spreading fire barely outside town, one of several that was to hit the Southwest that year with heartbreaking damage.

At the time, I was living in a small cottage awaiting the building of my home. That little abode was located in the mountainous, forested community where the fire started just outside a campground, but about a mile away at the opposite end of the same road. Not quite believing such a thing could be happening, I dashed to my car. I sped the short distance out of town on the highway toward my temporary home, only to be stopped by a roadblock. No one was being let in to the area.

That's when the realization that the event was real kicked in, and I flew back to my office in a panic to call my close friend Marilyn to help me find a way to get to the cottage. We thought we could get through from the other side of the wilderness area on old Forest Service roads. Thankfully, she agreed to drive since I was fast losing what composure I had maintained.

Apparently others had the same idea. We followed several cars, all bumping along as quickly as possible on winding, washboard and potholed roads. We were sheltered from the view of mushrooming smoke filling the sky by the tall pines, but we could certainly smell the destruction. A steady stream of vehicles stuffed with residents, their animal companions and belongings leaving the area in the opposite direction did nothing to steady me.

I had felt very fortunate when a friend let me move into his guesthouse at my decision to build. I'd decided that it was the perfect time to simplify my life. In my mind, I was looking forward to a Thoreau-esque existence for a number of months. The cottage may not have been on Walden Pond, but it was footsteps away from miles upon miles of ponderosa pines, alligator junipers and plentiful rock formations. I delighted in putting most everything I owned in storage to see just how sparsely I could live. It was a trial to see what I *really* needed. So those minimal aspects of my life that I had already deemed most important were contained in the place where I stayed and awaiting a fate unknown to me.

Uppermost and almost solely in my mind were the three cats who had deigned to live with me for many years. They had come to be so much a part of me and seen me through such a great deal that I didn't know how I would stand it to lose all three at once. As we raced through the forest, I was already steeling myself against a tragic outcome. But as we got closer, we got the sense that perhaps the fire hadn't yet advanced into the area we were going. Maybe there was a chance after all.

And, indeed, there was. When we rolled into the driveway and jumped out, we couldn't see any flames from where we were. We went straight to the task of corralling the cats and getting them into the car. This wasn't necessarily an easy feat, especially since Mr. Ambrose was still intensely skittish even after thirteen years. While Marilyn went to help my landlord contain a neighbor's dog for evacuation, I attempted to decide what else was important. I found that not much else was, except my writing notes, photography and altarpieces. But I started throwing clothing into sacks as well.

Returning along the same road, we came to a high point. I turned and looked back to see a ridge of flames leaping into the air and billowing smoke filling the sky. Watching the news after getting to her house, we saw that, blessedly for the residents of the little area where I stayed, the strong winds had chanced to shift in the opposite direction. Those homes were saved, but the forest and another housing area closer to town were not so fortunate. The fire had jumped the highway and quickly ignited all in its path. But we didn't need to watch the television to see what was happening. We could just stand in the backyard and view much of it, the slurry planes droning back and forth overhead and the flames getting closer. Then a miracle happened. The winds that had been wildly spreading the fire died down. In the next days we had some rain. Not a lot, but enough to slow things down. Within a few days the fire was contained, just blocks from the downtown area.

It was still to be several days before residents were allowed to return to the evacuated areas. That first night as I was settling down to sleep in my new temporary quarters at Marilyn's home, with the cats plastered to my side, I was extraordinarily grateful that I was not one of those who suffered a personal loss. I also felt soundly blessed that I had such a friend who was willing to rush madly with me into a potentially dangerous situation without any reservations. Everyone should be so fortunate.

But I was also aware that the entire town had shared in a deep soul-searching as to what really matters. Indeed, stories filled the newspaper and conversations for weeks. Handmade signs in shop fronts and driveways were evident proclaiming gratitude to the "Hot Shots" who had risked their lives to help us. That was before people seemed to forget the tragedy and returned to their normal lives.

However, I was left again with a real understanding of how transient everything is, how what we think permanent isn't, and the ways we attempt to avoid that knowledge. I reflected on the methods we use to try to cover up that truth by patching over it with layers of material goods, supposed entitlements and masked sentiments. This does nothing really other than enliven an underlying angst that we try to control by thrusting away the thoughts that continue to creep up on us. The threat of this real knowledge forces us into a denial that allows a shallow life and continued decimation of our natural resources as well.

The question that my dear friend and co-facilitator Daniel introduced during our recent retreat kept playing in my mind with added meaning. *Why do we wait?* Why do we wait to be who we really are? Why do we wait to express ourselves nakedly to those for whom we

76

care? Why do we wait to act in a way that says plainly, "I only have this present moment?"

When I first returned to the cottage, the surrounding air contained a shocked silence. There were no human voices, birdsongs or coyote calls. But strangely, there was something pristine in the burnt scent that hung in the atmosphere. In some ways it smelt of renewal to me. If renewal would gain a foothold, then I could somehow forgive the camper whose carelessness turned the wilderness into a moonscape and killed the forest dwellers or turned them out of their homes.

Several months later, when I held my monthly discussion forum, I focused on the subject of intent. I used Emma Cucchi's story as an example and also included a brief overview of the part that the coca leaf played in the Andes. After the rest of the circle shared some thoughts, we ended with a meditation. A few days later, I received a message from a newcomer to the sessions telling me how she appreciated the experience except for one thing. She said that I had essentially diverged from the subject matter into political grandstanding when I related the current threat to the coca leaf and what may be involved. I was astounded at her reaction and saddened as well.

It's not enough to say that we're not *actively* involved in perpetuating ruin. If we stick our heads in the sand, if we turn away because it's not "nice" to see, then *we* are just as guilty as those committing the crime. It's the cowardice of intentional naiveté and noninvolvement that continues to breed mindless havoc in our global and personal lives, all being essentially one anyway. Part of intent is being aware of what acts against it. It takes an impeccable courage to look everything head-on and see what is. Traveling starkly on the path will allow nothing else. It's about the activation and preservation of what is truly sacred.

The Essentials

There is something about death that brings things down to the essentials. The time that we thought was forever—isn't. We get down to the fact that we can't fool ourselves any longer. Because death had not yet touched me closely in my own life, I sought it out. I wanted to learn from it and, at the same time, be of what service I could with my limited understanding. I volunteered to be with those who were actively making the transition.

My first experience was one I will never forget and has colored the framework I've lived within ever since. I have much appreciation for the gift that a person I'll call Leslie gave me in allowing me to engage with her in the way she did, even though it was all too brief.

I was struck by the animation of her presence and delighted in the brogue in her speech, even through the resignation and tiredness that also surrounded her. She would regale me with stories of her days on the European stage many years prior. Unexpectedly, she would break into song. One time as our visit was ending, she struck a pose and said seductively, "A toute á l'heure!" Then, almost pirouetted her small frame and waved goodbye. Leslie spent much time with me going through photographs of friends where she used to live. It seemed very important to her that I know exactly who she was. She used the photographs to do so.

Then the truth of her condition began to sink into her mind and I saw the animation vacate. What came in its place was deep regret. She shared with me her anguish for a life not openly lived, and claimed she had never truly loved or been loved. One of the most difficult and yet one of the most meaningful things I have ever done was to merely sit and act as a presence—a witness—during the time she came to a kind of acceptance of her unfulfilled needs and unsung dreams. While I felt absolutely helpless at her grieving, there was something that knew more than I did advising me that trying to "make everything nice" and denying her this process would have been a grave error on my part. So, I set aside my own discomfort.

In an amazingly short time, there was a serene humility present more than anything else in her. One visit, I had the strange, overwhelming urge to kneel on the floor in front of her and wash her feet. I followed that internal prompting and asked if she would allow me not to wash them, but to massage them with cream. After some initial embarrassment and protestations on her part, she agreed. As she surrendered to the process, I bowed over her feet and allowed the incredible awe and deep emotion I was undergoing to guide my hands—because in that fragile, humbled personage I experienced the divine presence of Jesus.

Leslie passed within a few days. I'd had to travel out of town just prior and was walking alone under the night sky when I had a sense she'd released her body. I looked up into the mass of stars overhead and saw one that seemed to be twinkling brightly at me. I acknowledged her and then bade her peaceful travels.

It was very early in the morning. I was waiting sleepily in the agreed-upon parking lot for Daniel to pick me up. We were traveling together to attend a seminar, nearly a two-hour drive away. As he arrived and I slid into the seat, I greeted him and asked how he was.

"Not very well. I learned last night that Tim probably only has a short time now," he said softly.

I saw the grief in his eyes. Tim had been his closest friend for many years, the connection growing since they had met in graduate school. Even though families came along and work often intervened, they still maintained the bond that true friendship holds. A number of years ago, Tim learned he had brain cancer and had endured a number of treatments, remissions and recurrences.

After I determined with Daniel that it was really okay to continue on our way, he began driving southward. We were barely out of town when his breath expelled a barely contained sob, "I just regret that I never told him I love him!"

His despair wrenched at my heart, but I was certain of something that he wasn't acknowledging. Tim knew. It was not possible to be in Daniel's presence and not realize that he came from an inner place of lovingkindness. When I first encountered Daniel at a Zikr, a Sufi chanting circle for connecting with the Divine, I noted the energy preceding him into the room that spoke of his essence before I ever noted the person. That's when I determined I wanted to know him.

"Tim recognizes that you love him. How could he not? Maybe the outward expression of it is for you," I said.

He looked relieved. For the next couple of hours he told me about his feelings for Tim and his wife Cindy, and stories about all the synchronous ways their lives continued to come together over the years. He finished just about the time we pulled into the place where we would attend the workshop. The seminar turned out to be mediocre at best. My intuition was that the real reason for us to make the trip together had been finished just as we arrived at our planned destination.

A few days later, Daniel telephoned me. He said that Tim was gone and said how much gratitude he had to Cindy that she had willingly shared Tim's last hours with those who cared for him. She had called Daniel and told him that it was time.

As he recounted his experience in a joyous voice, on the other end of the phone line, tears streamed down my face. I could somehow see the light in his eyes.

"I was able to spend a good time alone with him. I sat with him and told him how I love him. I held his hand. I kissed his head. I sang to him." I made a picture in my mind of the two of them, one bending over the other, and heard Daniel's beautiful voice uplifted in a song of devotion, easing the transition for his friend.

"I don't know if he heard me or knew I was there."

Daniel, Tim knew.

Asceticism

It's the nature of movement toward the innermost Dwelling Places beyond Teresa's castle walls, or in upholding the Re-membering Process, to increasingly recognize and shed what is false. It's not only about what we deem untrue, but also what we determine has no relevance to the journey. It's not that there's anything particularly wrong with the irrelevant aspects themselves, it's that they no longer draw our attention or distract us from our chosen path. Mostly, those things belong outside the castle walls, or at least not much beyond the first couple of Dwelling Places.

We need to be alert to the fact that when we're no longer interested in buying the latest gewgaw or watching the next travesty on television, that it may get a negative response from others whom we have known who may be on a different wavelength than we are now. It's useful to recognize that when we may receive messages that we're about as fun as hardened mud, or we're denying ourselves the important things, that it's not asceticism in which we're engaging. It's a richer, deeper life.

In fact, the more such a person rants, the more we can understand that they wish to be inside the castle walls themselves, because asceticism is actually the denial of the divine inner life. At a certain level, the ranter recognizes that living a materialistic, shallow existence is actually inhabiting the parched desert of contained fear, but doesn't yet know how to move through the doorway toward something else.

As a way of beginning my work with people, I sometimes ask them to imagine that they have a short time to live and to decide what, if anything, they would do differently. It's not unusual for them to be fearful of engaging with my question. Are they afraid to look back on a life not fully lived? Leslie taught me the lessons related to that. Are they apprehensive about really expressing themselves? Daniel showed me the richness gained in being open. Are they torn about leaving others behind? We can uncover wider possibilities in service to them through our own discoveries. Maybe it's about the fear of the unknown beyond this material world. We have all been birthed from a former reality most of which we have forgotten. We will find the birthing canal on the far end as well. If we have lived intentfully, there will be no needed resolutions. We will have a good death from which to move easily on the next turn in the path.

Sometimes the "fires" in our lives allow the background—and what supports and nurtures us—to pop into the foreground. At the same time, it pushes the foreground—the noise with which we get distracted—into the background where it belongs. Mostly we don't get the message any other way than through the tragedies that happen in our own lives and the surrounding world. As mindless devastations continue to gain momentum around the globe and we admit to what is indeed transient, we must choose to hold the question: what matters? Then we must resolve to act on our answers.

CHAPTER SEVEN

The Space of No Need

A few years ago I traveled to Palenque, one of the largest excavated Mayan complexes located in the Mexican state of Chiapas, and to the jungles and towns of Belize. Some of those close to me may well have wondered what I was doing taking off on a trip of this nature at a most inconvenient, and perhaps even foolhardy time, considering the tenuous nature of my life from an outside perspective. Maybe if it was work-related they could have understood. More likely, I was projecting the questioning and judgments onto others when it was really that rational voice inside me that sometimes boomed forth and said, "What *are* you doing?" It turned out that it was indeed related to work, but of a deeper nature—the soul's work.

There was a strong calling within me that said I was to go, something so strong that I believed I would be very sorry if I listened to that logical part of myself that weighed the checks and balances, particularly in this case. I had no sense of why I was to go on this trip, or what I was to do while I was on it. However, I had no doubt that I would experience things that would strike a deep chord of realization within my being. So, in that state of *not knowing*, I set my core intent toward what I would learn from this journey and let it go.

In places like Palenque and Belize life slows down. The humidity and the soft energy of these rainforest spaces won't allow you to move too fast. In that lessening and more languid movement, distracting internal voices gradually hush. When silence is given space, elements of living you keep at bay are allowed to be fully present. Things we believe unreal or mystical begin to emerge.

That phenomenon was certainly true for me. Walking under the nearly full moon one night near the Mayan ruins of Palenque, the stars so bright and close I could nearly touch them, the canopy of the mountainous jungle black against the sky, I had the sense that I was walking in the midst of a vast canvas of art. Another night, I had a dream that played itself out in daylight reality within the next twenty-four hours. I began to understand that my companion and I were traveling with Grace, a guide often forgotten or blocked in our Western culture. She continued to be with us as we prepared to leave.

We were so immersed in our experiences that we made no plans exactly where we would go once we left Palenque. We had no reservations—of any sort. We didn't know how we would get to where we would go. About a day before we left, we did create a loose framework for Belize and found that even that vague structuring changed as we continued our travels—gratefully so.

Life became full of synchronicities that any well-laid plans would have put to rest. Without looking at schedules, we often rode on one bus just to get to our intermediate destination and step almost immediately on another one. When there was a seeming inconvenience, it was merely an intervention that led us to meet someone who directed us to an unusual spot or told us an incredible story. We rode the wave of unfolding that Grace provided. It was only in looking back—hindsight often being more clear—that I understood it was through setting our heart's intent and surrounding it with a warm permeable veil that we had "Indiana Jones" type experiences. This understanding led to the deeper meaning of my own function for this trip. By repeatedly being put in the midst of people or events that provided missing links for a story that had for a few years been on the back burner of my mind, my writing seemed to be one reason for the journey. But there was a much more important one. There were invisible shifts happening deep inside me that I couldn't name. The conscious realization I offer now is that when we learn to trust, we will be led to all we ever need. Our only job is to be awake and follow the lead. Having had the experience of this truth, I told my companion that I wanted to re-enter my daily life with this comprehension at a cellular level.

Contrast

The gods quickly complied, but not in the way I thought they would. Having departed Belize, we traveled up the coast of the Yucatan headed toward Cancun to catch our plane home. We stopped overnight in a little beach town and the magic of our trip continued. We met up with some friends we had left earlier in Palenque and reminisced about the first leg of our journey. Hoping to cross paths with these compatriots again soon, my companion and I separated from them. Thinking ahead to the long and early ride into Cancun the next morning to catch our plane, we choose to enter that big city to find overnight lodging.

From my point of view, the chrysalis immediately fell away. It appeared to me that I was in any large metropolitan city in the United States, except worse in that moment. Coming from the jungle, I was repulsed by the cacophony of horns honking, high-rise buildings and large retail chains on nearly every downtown corner. Clearly, tourism was king. But I couldn't understand why anyone would want to come there rather than stay home and experience the same confusion. I mourned for my peace.

The joke continued. We finally found a hotel and considered the price much too high. After having settled ourselves into our sixth floor room, we discovered the water in the bathroom ran in the shower, but not the sink. And electricity only emanated from one of the several outlets in the room. We were thankful that it was a bedside table.

Tired and needing to arise very early to catch our plane, I made an arrangement with the front desk for a wake-up call. Awaking with a start the next morning, I quickly realized that we had received no wake-up call and we were way behind schedule. Hurriedly throwing ourselves together, we went with our bags to the elevator. It no longer worked. While I flew down the six flights of stairs to pay the bill and find a taxi, my companion agreed to schlep our bags down.

We barely made our plane. But make it we did. And it set us down just in time to catch the Phoenix rush hour traffic, a treat in and of itself. We spent the next couple of hours driving northward to my home up in the mountains. The next day it snowed. I grumbled for days.

I was finally able to laugh after the fact. I realized that I was being tested—and hadn't necessarily passed the trial at the time. When we hold aversion in our minds we will continually be diverted. When there is no attachment, we will often be delighted. The ideal state to be in is the space of no need, where all experiences are equal places of learning and acceptance. I, of course, knew this lesson, but got to experience it again.

Some months later, some other companions of mine and I were offered the teaching once more, with a slightly different twist. We had all been working hard, too hard it turned out. I think often when any of us have had our noses too close to the computer, the wrench or whatever our tools of implementation, we tend to clamp down tightly around what we think will meet our needs—in any context. After all, there's just so much time and so much energy to be expended, so what we seek had better be within our short-sighted range of approval.

We decided to take three days and go on a camping trip. Three days would do it and home on the fourth—refreshed and ready to lean into the wind again. We resolved we would go to the White Mountains, a few hours east of our homes. There we'd find a wilderness place away from other people, with a running stream or placid lake, and miles of beautiful hiking opportunities. We wanted to engage in quiet and the restorative qualities of nature.

After the initial three-hour drive, then three hours beyond that, we were still driving around and around, ducking into this spot and that one. The driver was getting irritable. Not only was there no running water to be had since rain had been sparse in those parts that year, but it seemed like most of the wilderness seekers had in mind most of the areas that we sought. Besides, the dream place that one of us had remembered from a previous trip had vanished into time.

Instead, we found forests that appeared decimated with many logged trees downed, rocky ground that would provide uneven footing in hiking and too many other campers in the area for our taste. In a couple of hours it was going to be dark. We finally pulled into yet another forest road and parked, each setting off on foot looking for "the spot," even if only for the night.

We finally settled on a place, though not really happy about it. We set up our campsite, deciding that since we were there we might as well stay for the duration. It took us two days to finally get into the rhythm of the forest—an indication of something off balance to be sure.

By that time, we were able to appreciate the birds singing, the few coyotes at night and otherwise, the silence. There was the occasional ATV noise in the distance or other people going by on a nearby road, but after a while that didn't seem so important. And then we got our wish for running water. Torrential rains began to come down. Strangely, instead of getting upset about the whole thing we joked about being careful what you ask for.

We began to consider it all an adventure and rigged up a tarp for shelter, stringing it from the truck to nearby trees. We made a game of moving our camp chairs around to avoid the drips. We relaxed. And when we did, the magic happened.

We saw the beauty "even" in that forest and explored areas of our lives with each other that we hadn't touched on in a while, experiencing true community. We began to recognize how each of us had been wound up and figuratively depleted due to our own wrestling to control certain outcomes in our lives. And once again the Universe provided us exactly what we needed to be shown.

She provided us with the metaphor of our initial perceptions of the place where we stayed and the tight expectations we had to get each of us to look at our current autobiographies. The Divine has a wonderful way of mirroring what we hold within us, if we would only be alert. My companions and I caught on—again—and went home at peace.

Fresh Perspectives

There was a time in Berkeley when I talked to a group gathered to hear about my earlier book. I related to them some of my discoveries of the phases of the spiritual journey, other people's stories relative to these phases and insights coming from my own travels—usually but not always in exotic locales. After a guided meditation, I opened it up for discussion and questions.

"At least I was able to sit still during the meditation," this coming from a man seated in the front row. Then he looked dejected, "I see all these advertisements for these 'spiritual' trips to Egypt or Peru. You talk about going to India and all those other places. I can't even afford to get out of this city! How am I going to 'get enlightened'? Is it reserved for the rich? Do I have to travel?"

"That's a very interesting point." I was genuinely glad he asked the question. "I think you do have to travel. But not in the way you might think."

For any of us to evolve, we need to remove ourselves from what is familiar to us. If we can afford the luxury, perhaps the easiest way to do this is to take a trip periodically, particularly somewhere we haven't been, with a culture very different from our own. That doesn't mean the travel will be easy. In fact, sometimes when the travel is most difficult, fraught with problems, we have the best opportunity to learn about ourselves and perhaps what narrow lives we lead and the paralyzed mindsets we have. The opposite is also true. We can learn about previously hidden attributes that heretofore we hadn't exercised much. If we are open enough, we can grow through these experiences and return home.

The reality is, though, that many people don't have the financial resources to physically travel like that very often, or perhaps ever. In these cases, people who are able to travel beyond the familiar and expand, yet stay in their own backyards, are perhaps due much more of our respect. What is involved here is an uncanny ability to be one's own witness while immersed in the daily life.

My guess is that these folks have a much easier time of it with re-entry. The requirement for learning that way involves the ongoing ability to shift perspective momentarily to obtain a greater view and then go about their daily business with wider choices. While physical travel and contained retreat or workshop experiences create a safe cocoon for us to try out new thoughts and behaviors away from friends and family, we must learn ultimately how to effectively return home with our experimentations intact to integrate into our everyday reality. Otherwise our forays into the unknown are no different than continual mental and emotional masturbation.

One of the Big Questions

Sooner or later, traveling along the path of our own evolution, most of us come to the question of life purpose. For many of us this is a time of great teeth gnashing because we don't know our *raison d'être* and sense we aren't fulfilling it anyway. On the opposite end, we may do a lot of chest beating proclaiming our "mission" to the world, and spend a great deal of energy trying to get others to hear our message as they turn and run in the other direction. Likely, we will slide back and forth between the two extremes because we can't quite settle with either falsehood. This question of purpose is an age-old one, but maybe not with quite the twist it has had in our particular times.

Krista was a brilliantly intelligent woman of a certain age who had made a pleasant life for herself after coming out of earlier times that had a number of tragedies associated with them. She had a few irritations at work. But mostly these had to do with her own responses to others—she discovered—and her tendencies to want all to be perfect according to her own judgment. Otherwise, she had a beautiful long-time intimate relationship that fit wonderfully for her. And she had the means to do most of what really meant something to her. Yet, she experienced an incredible fatigue and great gut-wrenching spiritual angst that tore at her continually. She felt abandoned by God and betrayed by her Core Self.

"Life is so hard. I'm like Sisyphus pushing the boulder uphill. I almost get to the top when something happens and the boulder rolls over top of me and drags me all the way down to the bottom again."

She felt as though she wasn't doing what she was put here to do and didn't know what that something was anyway. As we all have, Krista had her own special circumstances of living and the mind's interpretations along the way that developed outlooks and life beliefs about self and the world in general. In her case, no wonder she was so tired and spiritually anguished when she tormented herself with an ongoing, albeit mysterious, lack.

I can't help but think that some of the current New Age philosophies that seduce our egos by touting grandiose life designs may have contributed to her sense of failure and frustration. Maybe it's because we live in an age of transformation and recognize that we are likely fast rushing toward some kind of genesis that will take us through the threshold to another way of living. It seems it must happen like that if the global community continues to consume the way it has. Or perhaps it's because the story of the Messiah returning to this physical plane of existence is so ingrained and we have limited interpretations of the prophecy.

There is a preponderance of self-proclaimed avatars out there today hell-bent on saving the world when all any of us can really do is to heal ourselves. Siddhartha didn't start out thinking he would be the Buddha. He had his own torments to uncover. The same must have been true for the person known as Jesus—who later became the consciousness called Christ. The times before His ministry are kept secret from us. Any of us have the choice to take the figurative trip into the desert to spend the forty days and nights it sometimes takes to spark the illumination that even allows us to be aware of the castle doorway leading to hidden Dwelling Places.

This is the journey that brings us back to our true identity. If we think our purpose is anything other than that undertaking, then we are being misguided by following the lead of our own inflated ego. Once we reconcile ourselves to this understanding, life gets easier in many ways because we learn that it's *not* about external striving, but inner attunement.

We can relax to the interior expedition over which we have complete control in the depth and breadth of its unfolding. Or do we? After we've surrendered the reins, the Universe may accelerate the trip, showing us again what the real ride is about.

The process of our lives will create the content of our fulfillment. The outcome of our learning then is the real gift that we can share with others just by virtue of reflecting inner light. For Krista, she finally realized this law and determined, "*Being* is enough."

CHAPTER EIGHT

Conflicts on the Path

I was distraught. I could not imagine how I now found myself in such a distressful, heart-breaking situation. While I experienced every other aspect of my life to be aligned with spiritual intent and practice, how could it be that I was enduring such terrible sadness and disappointment in this part?

After undergoing exponentially increasing discomfort, the thick tension finally manifested itself in my body as stabbing pain. It continually visited me in the middle of the night when there were no distractions from the day. I recognized that I was being given an insistent message that I preferred not to receive.

I was forced to look past the possibility that things would change to the reality that they would not, and could even get worse. I knew that I had to take an action I never dreamed I would have to take. And for the parties concerned, I needed to do it very soon. I fretted, the question about the right time being on my mind for weeks.

One morning, beleaguered with the need to act and the last vestiges of hope asking me to stay the action, my mind swirling and heart heavy, I seemed pulled to the forest by some unknown power. Walking the short distance to the entrance, I already began to feel a letting go. Once there, each footfall placed meditatively on the earth sent my anguish into the earth to be composted. The sun's heat coming to me through the tall trees entered my skin, bringing me the sustenance needed, replacing the heaviness. My breath automatically began to support the process. On the inhalation, glowing warmth moved into the cells of my body. On the exhalation, grief vacated.

Then I suddenly had the overwhelming urge to sing. There in the middle of the forest with no one but wilderness residents to witness, I began to intone, softly at first, then full voice.

La Illaha Il Allah Hu!

Over and over again, still hiking steadily, I sang the Sufi chant with which I was so familiar.

There is nothing but God! There is no reality but God!

Just as the sun's radiation replaced the burdens I felt in my body, so the true meaning of the line I had sung so many times before entered the cavity left in my mind and heart where desolation and confusion had dwelled just a short time ago.

Everything is God! Even the difficult trial I was encountering was Divine! As this deep realization sprang from the unconscious depths of my mind, I simultaneously felt my heart center open. Tears, not of despondency, but of joy, coursed down my cheeks. I felt a sense of great peace and strength even in the face of the situation that still existed.

Still basking in the afterglow, I returned home. And with a deeper wisdom informing my thoughts, I immediately took the needed action as gently as I knew how to do.

Cleaning House

A woman once told me about a significant dream she'd had during a time when she was undergoing a forced transition. Upon awakening, still seething with anger, she clearly remembered every detail.

94

She found herself in a large house with many rooms. It was crawling with workmen. Unbeknownst to her, her home was being remodeled. All manner of things were being dismantled and exposed. Ductwork and carpeting was being replaced. Secret alcoves were being divulged. Wild colors like chartreuse were being splashed on the walls.

She tracked down her mother who happened to be there and said, "What's going on? I didn't authorize this! We're supposed to be partners in this enterprise! Nobody ever tells me anything!"

"Oh, we need to have this done and we have a little money put aside."

"How much?"

"We have $3.5 million."

She overheard some workmen chuckling conspiratorially that the work was going to take five times that amount of money.

One of them came up to her and said, "Things would go a lot better if your father would come out and engage with the workers."

Searching for her father, she found him off in a corner, hiding away from everyone else, reading a newspaper. About that time, she awoke.

Often, dreams involving houses metaphorically equate with the self—the make-up of our life, psyche or body. When she spoke of the meaning pertinent to her, she suggested the same. She recognized her father's isolation as her own. And also acknowledged a probability that the fear and resentment that she allowed to inhabit her mind had lent themselves to the manifestation of a cancer in her body.

She comprehended that the dream was showing her what she needed to release and to take part actively in her own healing process. Perhaps the large dollar amounts signified the energy and focus she unconsciously thought it would take to create the prescribed alterations in thought and lifestyle patterns.

It's easy to become overwhelmed at this point, give up and retreat. The constraining arms of the past snatch us back just as we are walking the edge, contemplating freedom. And we succumb to what we knew instead of trusting what we don't know. We try to go back to sleep. For most of us, there is no real rest, but a state of fitfulness. Ultimately we cannot ignore the message we've been given. If we do so, our soul suffocates, finally dying.

Thus, there comes a time when we are knowingly left with the ramifications of the choices we make. While it would be comforting to think that the progressions we undertake will be painless and smooth, any change involves conflict between what was and what will be. Therein lies the opportunity for learning and alignment to an authentic life.

It doesn't mean that we were intentionally leading a false existence. Mostly we were taught to conform. In conforming, we gave up parts of ourselves, parts that wanted expression. Instead, those aspects found voice in muffled mourning, acted out through fear of going against the grain, culminating in heaviness of various sorts.

We can gauge the measure of truth in our lives by the lightness of our body, emotions and energy. We need only be aware in any given moment of the state of our being, and be guided. This is what we are asked to do on the spiritual path. We aren't headed for a continuing chaotic free fall, but an order of Divine nature.

In the progression, we most often dance back to what was and forth to what will be. We certainly face the confliction strongly as we venture inside Teresa's castle and enter the first couple of Dwelling Places. With each dance step we perhaps allow the foot forward to rest a little bit longer, gaining familiarity and comfort there before submitting to the temporary step backward. We are also called upon to become, if not comfortable, at least tolerant of the conflicts we find in the transition. It's this willingness that serves our evolution. We then move more easily through the next few rooms of the castle, by now being somewhat knowledgeable of the layout.

But we finally face the ultimate treaty when, in the most interior rooms, we discover what we are, in truth, asking of ourselves—the obliteration of the self in order to pass into Unity. Only a few make this great negotiation.

Most of us who get this far hover on the razor's edge, desiring, not yet surrendering. We're unable to see the doorway because we are blind to it. It's difficult to discern through a veil of hesitancy or fear. Who could blame any of us for wobbling on the path at this point? We don't know for sure that a resurrection *does* take place and that we *do* return to a larger life.

For each entrance we cross, whether initially beyond the castle's exterior walls, or the ensuing rooms within, we will cycle through the Re-membering Process. To gain some ease, we first need to recognize the dynamics. It's the ongoing interplay of chaos and order, conflict and resolution, moving and resting. With the transition from one phase to another, one room to another, a certain amount of conflict happens, internally or externally, that signals us of the need to clean our house, to open the door to other experiences—and deepening, if we're discerning. Opportunity comes most often through the chaos that breaks out, the creative spurt, the unsettling of sensibilities. But in the best focus of heart and mind—during Sparking, Separation and Search—we navigate through the chaos, finding what best serves the journey. We then discover an obvious order in Initiation before we enter a more ordered chaos in Re-Entry.

Then we cycle through again, but find the process more comfortable in its familiarity through the same territory, yet different ground. This is the ingrained nature of the path.

Guidance of the Heart

During the large portion of my life when I was heavily weighted in my head, a strange phenomenon would sometimes occur. Periodically I would feel uneasiness in my body, usually in what is known as the Solar Plexus region, or diaphragm area. It wasn't a pain, but some kind of energetic turbulence, even though I wouldn't have known enough to describe it that way at the time. My mind would note the discomfort, but would be literally clueless to the cause and ignore it. I'd continue engaging in whatever I was doing without knowing that it was that very thing that was generating the response in my body.

The activity usually involved a relationship of some sort where I was unconsciously choosing not to recognize some dynamic that didn't serve me. Oftentimes, it had to do with an old behavior of mine related to being fearful of stating my own needs. I'd let things go along hoping that all would somehow turn itself around and that person would hear my silent requests and comply with them. Needless to say, that didn't happen and was most detrimental toward one of my highest values—honesty.

At different points, it was as though a part of me had had enough of this playacting. This "honest" part always chose a time when I was relaxed with the person, after a nice dinner or sitting in front of a fire. Suddenly, a true pronouncement of the situation and any misalignment in our relationship would leap out of my mouth, very matter-of-fact, but never hurtful. The person I was with would be as astounded as I was. It was as though an invisible third party was present and we didn't know who it was.

The words would hang in the air awaiting scrutiny, mine and the other person's, and were then the impetus for candid conversations, ones we really both desired anyway in order to come clean. What would follow for me was an absolute clarity about being true to myself. It was about a direct comprehension toward what best

98

served me, in order to walk a higher path, and the sometime hard decisions that came as a result.

Life being the learning curve that it is for me, I still revisit old thought forms and behaviors every now and then. But I'm much more astute than I was back then due to some painful lessons. When something is uneasy in my body, my Witness is much more apt to kick in to kindly and objectively alert me to any straying from integrity to myself that I may be doing. I've learned to listen and act accordingly, even though perhaps dragging my feet like a child told to undertake a disliked chore.

The heart's wisdom holds intent and recognizes what aligns with it. If we weren't taught to devalue the resident Mystery that resides within us, the knowing that comes from that place would automatically enrich our minds, informing our decisions. As it is, logic and unhealthy desire often take its place and rationale becomes the heavy, pointing out the direction to take. And how the mind can rationalize when the ego is insistent!

When the heart's message goes unheard, its connecting circuitry dammed, it naturally seeks another conduit to carry the message. Finding the body and the subtle energy field as cooperative partners, it often launches its communiqué through these means. Most of us being unused to paying attention to these terminals need to school ourselves to be consciously aware in order to receive the dispatch.

It has been through tutoring myself in awareness of the indications in my body and subtle energy field that I have come to be guided best. It's been a matter of listening to the silent commands of the heart that continually show me the way. How encrusted the internal line of communication has become will determine how cleanly the guidance is presented for any of us. Sometimes if the passageway is too narrow and thorny, the heart must gather momentous strength and ramrod the instruction through the obstructions. This way it overrides the mind's logic or excuses and catapults us into an action of some sort. This can look like impulse, something not clearly decided—particularly to others. Instead of rashness, in this case it's actually a deep consideration coming from the still point. If not fully engaged, intent is always hovering nearby awaiting the opportunity to interject what will fulfill it.

The cleaner we are, by clearing illusions and limitations generated by the ego self, the more awareness we have of the heart's intelligence. The gentle prodding of intuition will then be the escort leading us on the evolutionary path.

Even so, followers of intuition may still be met with suspicion by parts of themselves and with scrutiny from others. The internal and external tribes typically stay within the confines of habit and what is familiar in order to perpetuate survival, even if it's not truly safe or even useful.

My own biggest leaps in consciousness and subsequent richer life have ensued by going against the grain, stepping outside arbitrary learned rules, whether mine or someone else's. During those times, rather than listening to the analytical, lawful voice, I've chosen to adhere to the code of the outlaw, knowing completely that by doing so I will break out of confinement.

The trick, of course, is to be able to recognize when the outlaw is actually a benefactor instead of some trespasser looking to lead me off on the rabbit trail of distraction. This becomes a skill learned over time and through experience toward the signal given. For myself, it's been a practice of focusing inward and becoming aware of the location of the source of instruction. If an image or internal message comes from a point in my upper right visual field, I know I can trust it. If it comes from some other direction, particularly from the left, I know it's somehow a detractor. This is my own personal awareness of my internal workings that have proven out over time. It may be different for others, but the knowledge of such is easily accomplished merely through honing perception.

The Promise of Light

When most of us begin wading in the watery depths of spiritual consciousness, we have no idea what's ahead. If we did, we might well jump with lightning speed out of the pool and quickly towel off our feet trying to pretend they hadn't been wet at all. But the cool sweetness of the initial waters is as seductive as the hormones released when we fall in love that make us crazy, losing any thought of what may come after the honeymoon period is past. Instead, we retain the notion of "happily ever after" until the road becomes uneven and too rocky, and yet still we insist on holding onto the fairy tale for a while longer.

The great cosmic conspiracy that ensnares novice travelers is the promise we think is extended that says the journey will only be full of love and light. There is no such pledge. However, we do unknowingly make a covenant. We have light's promise that its other side shall be exponentially present as well.

Typically, we don't like to enter into the darkness. We don't know how vast it is. The outlines aren't clear. Since we don't know the form, we can only imagine how monstrous it must be. Through imagination, a demon of darkness can well grow huge in proportions to the little troll it may really be. Rather than taking the chance to check it out, most of us prefer to keep it grated below the landscape. That way it doesn't escape and get out of control. So, we tread overhead keeping it contained. But every now and then, it reaches through the bars as we pass by and successfully grabs an ankle, thereby proclaiming its presence and demanding our attention. When that happens, we're usually horrified at the warty, putrid smelling hand it exhibits and desperately try to shake free of its grip. But it only latches on more furiously, now a manacle that stops our progress abruptly. Or does it?

I was raised to be accepting of people. Even in childhood, I can remember an ability to experience the essence of others beyond any persona that was presented. It didn't mean that I necessarily always liked the behavior, but could appreciate the person behind it. Later, this trait became part of my spiritual practice and my capacity toward compassion seemed to deepen greatly. As with any virtue, if taken to an extreme, it can be detrimental as well. I had to take a look at how acceptance could range into endurance and a negation of myself. Over time, I have come to be more in balance and realize that part of honoring others is also to honor myself. My connections and sense of sacred community expanded as a result.

Then came what I considered to be a major setback. Someone who I felt was very dear came to participate peripherally in the community that had begun to gather around our common intent of spiritual opening. At first, her hopes for a deeper sense of peace seemed truly present, even though she behaved in overly self-effacing and unhealthy ways. But the fire was too hot. Or the environment felt safe enough to expose previously hidden sides. It appeared to me as though her backsliding was moving into an avalanche that was going to bury her. In the course, she was projecting blame, especially toward me. A part of her cried out for help while the more vocal part wanted nothing of the sort and railed against it. The behavior was crazy making. I was not only sad about this situation, but also greatly frustrated.

I began to find that I was having judging thoughts about her. I'd push them away and return to recognizing what pain she must be experiencing for her to generate such conduct. But the more I chose to ignore my own responses, the more they began to arise. In my mind, unflattering images of a cartoon character began to surface in reference to her. I was ashamed to be thinking in this manner. Yet, as her behavior worsened, not only did these thoughts loom in the foreground, but I also took what measures I could to absent myself when she was around. I did make a few attempts to talk with her about what was poisoning our environment. However, these encounters ended rather quickly as I sensed real physical danger present.

Finally, a separation occurred. We were no longer in each other's presences at all, nor did she have any contact with our community. The circle closed, covering what space she'd left. When that happened, I felt an incredible relief as though some heavy armor had vacated my soul. The internal tension of staying any thoughts that weren't "nice" or loving must have relaxed because what had been trapped below came out with a vengeance. I felt revulsion. At a chance encounter, I found that I literally could not look at her. It was as though, if I had done so, I would have gotten physically ill. I was horrified that I was experiencing such emotions. Never in my entire life had such intensity of this sort occurred. And I still tried to stuff the feelings back into whatever hole from which they'd emerged. But having found an escape hatch, this vehemence wasn't going to be repressed any longer.

I awoke in the middle of the night. I lay there for a while, fully present. The darkness was still and my sleep had been untroubled as far as I knew. But through the window of silence, without any conscious thought, loathing engulfed me. Waves of nausea moved through me. It wasn't even object-focused. It was as though I was surrounded by a leper colony, the worst suffering of humankind, clawing at me, intent on bringing me down. I could feel myself trying to shrink, to skitter away. Silent screams were ricocheting in my head. Suddenly, a message came through. "Be still. *Be* with it."

Even as every instinct was telling me to leap out of bed and turn on the light, I forced myself to remain stationary. I consciously released the contraction in my energy field, body and mind. And when I did so completely, the heaviness dispersed, the impermeable shield no longer there. Light returned without the use of the traditional bulb.

Years ago I had a professor who said, albeit in more graphic terms, that in every pile of manure there was a nugget of gold. Perhaps just because it was shocking to me to hear that rather staid-looking woman make such an earthy statement in an academic environment, the phrase stuck with me. I've also come to find that it's true, not through a Pollyanna attitude, but from one of learning and growth. We need only to look for the jewel in even the most difficult situation and allow it to open the way before us.

What does it mean to be a spiritual being? For most of us, it means maintaining expressions of kindness, compassion, unconditional love, and complete surrender. It's also about being present, perhaps in a way not often practiced. In most spiritual traditions, beatific attitudes are emphasized. We're given the thought that anything else is unacceptable. It we take this as true, then the internal critic will have a field day when we think uncharitable thoughts.

In reality, the brighter the light, the darker the shadow will also be, maybe just stored in the deeper realm of consciousness. The practice of being present is recognition of both aspects inside each of us, and the gradations in between. When we fight against anything, it just looms larger than it needs to be. An understanding of what truly dwells in the interior places of all humankind, *including* ourselves, tends to level the playing field.

It has become hard for me to induce spiritual egoism with a knowledge that if a heavy emotion has been triggered it's because what someone else is displaying is also resident inside me. Sometimes only through feeling like a fraud can true compassion and humility be instilled—for all concerned.

Missionary Work

This then becomes the profound practice that conflict can bring. It's the willingness to face the wounded, unacknowledged parts of ourselves that we find through any incongruence we have allowed over time. Indeed, how does the regular appearance of a particular incongruence actually show that a part of us is overly ripe for healing?

A measure of where we are in our own evolution becomes the point where a split takes place. We somehow stand outside our own thoughts or actions and watch, fully aware of the mismatch to where we want to be. Yet, we engage with it anyway. This becomes the hint that we are in the phase of awareness, the first step to transformation. The old habit will begin to fall away. And reintegration will occur.

We will continue to bump up against others and ourselves when there is a misalignment. Even if we've been traveling quite some time, any old residue that would block our progress will be presented to us in the needed form in order to be appreciated and released. In fact, collisions may become even more drastic and dramatic just because the investment of intent is greater to remove anything that would insult it. And the missionary work of conflict provides the tool for the soul's learning.

CHAPTER NINE

The Edge of Limitation

I had been leading the group in our opening meditation, the one that encouraged each of us to leave whatever we had brought with us of our day outside the door—to create a sacred space. After looking around the circle and seeing that everyone had returned from their "emptying" process, I announced the open frame. This is the part of our gatherings where I invite anyone who would like to do so to share something of a personal nature pertaining to their spiritual development, or to ask a question. Several people shared their challenges and progress. Then there was silence. Silence being a powerful generator, I allowed it to gel for a few minutes. Out of the stillness came the voice of one of those assembled, directing a question to me.

What is the edge of limitation?

The depth of the query startled me. It wasn't because I thought the person asking to be incapable of such. Quite the contrary. It was the koan-like nature of the question. My remembrance is that I gave an answer at the time that spoke to the limitlessness of the Core Self. But even as I spoke I acknowledged that I had eschewed real clarity in favor of offering *something* to the questioner. However, it instituted the particular inquiry that I continued to surface in our circle in different ways over time, and that I remain sitting with today. My sense is that it's a quest for each of us to determine our own meeting point between limitation and freedom.

It's also important to realize the tension created where what seem like polarities join. In actuality, we could liken this display of thought and no thought to works by the late Abstract Expressionist Mark Rothko. Rothko explored the relationship between complements by placing large squares or rectangles next to each other on canvas, usually those hues opposite on the traditional color wheel. Where the two came together there was a shimmering effect and they fuzzed out and became indistinct at the edges, each merging into the other. Therefore, one informed the other. On the canvas called the spiritual path, we can draw an analogy to the veil between two worlds that really begins to overlap as we progress in our awareness.

Meeting Points

There is an old Sufi story about a lion cub that became separated from the pride. As the lion cub was wandering lost and crying, some sheep noticed him and took him in as one of their own. They taught him to think, walk and talk as a sheep. A few years later, it happened that another lion came upon this same sheep herd. While considering a tasty meal, he noticed a younger lion in their midst. The younger lion was *baaing* like a sheep while *grazing*!

The older lion was appalled. He thundered in and dragged the younger one by his sprouting mane over to a pond, shoving his face over the water. "You're not a sheep! You're a lion like me—majestic and courageous! Not some crying thing examining the tail in front of him or the ground below his face!" With that, the older lion let loose an immense roar.

That revelation and its punctuation excited, yet confused the younger lion and he let out something between a *baa* and a yelp. But over time and with the guidance of the older lion, who helped him to reach inside himself, the younger lion began to roar.

The split second we attach ourselves to the physical body during the birthing process into a material world, we feel the existential pain of separation. One of my close friends told me an astounding story about his nephew. The incident happened during a family gathering when his nephew turned two years old. The two of them were alone in the little boy's bedroom playing with toys when my friend asked him, "What was it like when you were born?" The little guy pulled a chair over to the wall, just under the light switch. He proceeded to clamber up onto the support and flip the light off and on several times exclaiming in his baby voice, "Cold! Cold!" When asked the same question by my friend a few years later, the five-year-old didn't remember.

Most of us spend our lives trying to reconnect with what we intuitively know is there. But we get befuddled just like the young lion, because the farther from our birth date we get, the less we remember our original face. Due to our forgetfulness and inexperience, we allow others to fit a face of their making over our own that anchors itself in the mind to hold it in place. The problem is that sheep, even though well intentioned, have been through a similar homogenization process themselves.

While it may be useful to experience "sheep-ness" to some degree to understand the parameters of that particular pasture, it's the Core Self, inherent within us, who knows the geology of the entire terrain. If we're able to incorporate that deeper knowledge back into the pastureland, or animal husbandry, now *that's* something about which to roar!

The challenge is that our sheep selves are most likely by that time fixated on individual blades of grass, where we believe we gain our sustenance. Occasionally during the grazing process, we may have some notice that our growing paws seem out of place amongst tracks left by cloven hooves. But we quickly divert our attention so as to deny the fact. Sometimes it takes someone or something outside ourselves to drag us over to a mirror and say, "Look!" Even then, we may refuse to acknowledge who is really there. It would mean moving out of the pastureland. And we remember the angst separation brought before.

Where is the meeting point between complacency and possibility?

Some people need to be shown the mirror over and over before they then begin to move toward integration. A number of years ago, I worked with Nina, a very dear woman who had been badly hurt early in life. While she did the best she could to keep the pain at bay, it naturally kept resurfacing because what is registered in our minds we continue to resurrect in various ways, whether in memory, or through circumstances and others with whom we engage.

Even though she didn't acknowledge it herself, her sweet innocence and purity were plainly visible to me. My awareness made it that much more difficult for me to hear her continually berate herself.

Finally I said to her, "See yourself through *my* eyes. I *see* your purity, who you are." She looked at me through tears, rejecting my version of her. But over time, as I continued to tender the invitation, the communication of her eyes progressed from disbelief to doubt, hope—and then acceptance. It was a true joy to witness Nina's evolutionary journey, the one that carried her original face to a resting place of honor that now conveys itself through her glowing smile.

Where is the meeting point between pain and healing?

I have a round face. It's not nearly as round as it used to be, likely due to the number of years I've worn it. But when I was a child, it was decidedly round and its unsuspecting shape was the source of much of my suffering. My early school years are mostly a blur, but the times I do remember with crystal clarity were when my classmates used to taunt me, one boy even spitting in my face. "Pumpkin head! Pumpkin face!"

That was not the kind of notice I wanted at all, if any. I withdrew around other children for the most part, preferring to be around adults or alone with my own company, becoming painfully shy.

There was evidence of this transition in my childhood pictures. Early photos showed a bright-eyed, happily inquisitive child who sometimes appeared to be seeing something beyond the setting in which she posed. Once I entered school and stretching into the years ahead, the pictures shifted dramatically to that of a deadly serious girl, looking mistrustingly at the camera, probably because it would capture the features she thought had betrayed her. I considered myself lacking and unacceptable to others and myself in my supposed difference. There was also a part of me that knew better, the one who embraced her parents' love and filial pride.

In my twenties, I even worked part-time for a while as a runway model and did a local television commercial or two in my unconscious attempt to show myself that my physical presence was favorable. That endeavor, of course, proved to be an oxymoron, the industry itself being fraught with mixed messages that can instill even further doubt. Fortunately, it didn't take long for my deeper sensibilities to be horribly appalled at the plastic and sometime vicious nature inherent in that field. I left the exploration and took my lack of confidence with me unappeased.

In reality, what child hasn't undergone teasing and bullying to some extent? For some reason that I cannot determine, I internalized the hurtful messages at an extreme level. Even as an adult, when someone would innocently comment on the shape of my face, I would flinch. It's only been in the last several years that this former shame has transformed itself. And it was through a series of synchronous events placed closely in time that I came to relate to a deeper aspect of myself coming to me through my heritage. That reinterpretation freed me.

It started one spring when I attended hypnotherapy training. During an experiential portion, I was paired with an older Navajo man. It was my turn to guide him in a trance process. I have no recollection of the nature of the work or the words I uttered, but I vividly recall his response. Upon returning to the present moment, he looked at me and cried ecstatically, "How did you know to lead me to the fire?"

Whatever happened during his reverie seemed to have profound meaning to him, but it was more likely his interpretation of the language I used than any directed command on my part. However, over the next day or so, I noticed him periodically watching me from a distance. Finally, he approached me.

"Can I ask you a personal question?" There was something incredibly humble in this man's demeanor that endeared him to me. After I gave him permission, he continued, "Do you have Indian blood?"

I affirmed his question, but was astounded that he could see beyond my blue eyes and very light complexion and hair. "How did you know?" I was curious how he could discern that fact, the full-blooded portion down my mother's line being four generations removed from me. I hadn't thought much about that part of my lineage since she had told me when I was eleven years old.

He gave me a quiet smile and said, "It's the way you speak and the way you move." Somehow, his ability to *see* and acknowledge me in that way, beyond the surface presentation, was very important to me. It was as though he had, in turn, led me toward a kind of purification fire. It seemed to leverage an opening of some sort inside me, even more so than I conceded at the time.

Less than two months later, I was in Aspen for a couple of weeks. When I first arrived I had noticed an announcement in the newspaper for a showing of Edward Curtis' photography in a local gallery. It caught my attention at the time because I was fascinated with black and white photography. But I didn't know where the gallery was and made no effort to find out.

About a week later, I had made an appointment to get my hair trimmed at a salon in the village and right afterward was to proceed to a cranial sacral session. Because I didn't know where the stylist was located, I set out well before my appointment. Strangely enough, it turned out that the gallery displaying Curtis' works was right next door to the salon. I also had a good length of time to spare before my haircut. So, I entered. The entire upstairs of the gallery was devoted to the exhibit and I was the only one there.

In the silence and through Curtis' genius, I was drawn into his photographs. I lingered in front of each one examining them in detail, as though they all had some connection, something to say, to me. Indeed, it seemed as though something was building as I moved from one to the other, witnessing the quiet dignity and sometime stark beauty in the images of the Indian peoples from long ago that he captured on paper. Then, I noticed the very round shapes of many of their brown faces, just like my own—and I stood stock-still. Suddenly a voice came from my right, materializing out of thin air, and said firmly, "It's time to remember our heritage." I didn't recognize the voice, but its message generated a kind of internal solidity that hadn't been there before.

Glancing at my watch, I realized I was late for my haircut and reluctantly turned to leave. Even though keeping such a mundane appointment seemed ludicrous to me at the time, given the deepening I had just undergone, I went. From there I had just enough time to make my cranial sacral session. I was to find that the experience wasn't yet completed.

I have told some of what was to follow in my previous book *Calling Our Spirits Home*. For perhaps a couple of years, I'd had intense pressure at the base of my skull when meditating, like a plug in a dike wanting to blow. What I now know is that I'd had a blockage there that had kept my Third Eye from opening.

I'd made the acquaintance of Aspen herbalist Todd Welden the previous year. A truly gifted practitioner, he also did cranial sacral and somatic release work. I'd had a sense that he was the one to help me with the pressure. Indeed, he'd barely touched the back of my head one time and asked me if I'd incurred an injury, perhaps even during birth. I hadn't, confirming that fact with my mother, or during any other time to my recollection. But emotional injury can certainly be lodged in the subtle energy field or the physical body. I'd also had an intuitive understanding for a long time that the spot where pressure built at the back of my head was a place that certain knowledge entered. I had the thought that the entry point had been blocked at my birth for some obscure reason.

Todd had put me on the table and moved my physical body in certain ways. Then, he stationed himself behind me and barely tapped the back of my skull. When he did so, I began to have multiple, clear images of ancient Native faces moving swiftly across the movie screen of my mind's eye. Then, gut-wrenching despair started to surface, even though I did everything I could to hold back. I normally subdued such intense feelings. But his kind voice assured me it was perfect to let it go. And the floodgates opened. I had never felt such acute emotional pain. I released it with wracking sobs that came from some place beyond any experience I could have imagined. After a time my grief subsided, and with it something flew away. The space previously blocked was wide open.

The anguish had been such that I questioned if it was mine alone. We often carry with us what was sent down the generational line, even though unintentionally. Perhaps it was that the healing I'd experienced was shared with all of my ancestors, no matter their cultural origins. I hoped so. Whatever the case, it's my belief that my Native forbearers have been making their presences known to me ever since. Even now after all this time, I regularly smell tobacco burning, as though during ceremony. Usually, it happens during my meditations. But sometimes I smell the rich scent during walks in the forest. There are also times when it wafts through during the normal course of my day. I feel my roots. They comfort me. And I find strength there.

Where is the meeting point between forgetting and remembering?

The Holy Grail

For most of our lives we search for those things outside ourselves to inform who we are. A natural tendency toward doing so exists because we first knew of ourselves through others and the surrounding environment. We began to develop an identity as children, through external messages that we ingested. But that's about the development of the personality and also learning accepted methods for navigating in a material world.

The acknowledgement of our Core Self is another matter, and one to overlay the everyday self. If we allow ourselves to know the boundless aspect that carries us, we will entrain our lives with all eternity.

We get off track on the journey when we believe that the Divine lives outside us. How could we not be permeated by All That Is? It's contradictory to think otherwise. Indeed, it may even be considered blasphemous, although there's no need for anyone to be struck down, just opened. We could make the decision to hold Divinity outside ourselves, leaning out farther and farther for the golden ring that never quite comes within reach. But we *could* make the choice to allow that Presence to emanate from our innermost dwelling place to the outermost point of our everyday lives.

We regain this hidden knowledge through an appointment we make—the one with intent. It's that lightning strike, invoked through the crown of the head, which pierces the bowl of the pineal gland. Then the charge travels down the glandular channel of the upper chakras, the energy centers, to cleave the covering of the foundational place of the heart. Thus discovered, the heart first smolders. But presently its enraptured beating ignites a blaze that will infuse our lives.

We are broken open. There was never any informing to be done. The mold was made in Infinity and the substance that would fill it was poured into the interior cavity of our being before we were even born. What we thought lost and stolen was not just the radical magic of the pineal cup, but also the knowledge of its secret support and resting place in the heart. And we find that the Holy Grail was within all along. The search is now over. The integration can begin.

Where is the meeting point between parallel worlds and infused existence?

Distinctions

We all have our own spiritual research to undertake. It may be about the personality and its residential landscape, but the distinctions made will be about the internal Infinite. In our exploration, we can look to the common threads that run through our lives and point toward our particular affinity for speculative learning.

Where is the meeting point between self-doubt and humility?

Where is the meeting point between denial and recognition?

Where is the meeting point between pity and compassion?

Where is the meeting point between control and surrender?

Where is the meeting point between loneliness and solitude?

Where is the meeting point between withholding and intimacy?

Where is the meeting point between aversion and acceptance?

Where is the meeting point between fear and distinction?

The outcome of this scrutiny will be the finely honed attunement of the tensions we hold. Perhaps we will allow the overlay to occur that will dissolve any separation. The edges will cease to exist. The energy of the threshold will carry itself. We will know That which lies beyond the doorway to be ours.

CHAPTER TEN

Asking the Answer

Each time we return with a practice or ceremony to a physical space, or even time of day, we continue to collect the energy generated there. The method and place where we engage becomes the storehouse that increases the strength of the ritual and the gateway of spiritual development.

We know this to be the case due to the various sacred spots in the world, known as power places. Many of these locales are associated with ley lines, or strong energy meridians naturally existing in the earth. Over the centuries, people were drawn to these locations instinctively and built their temples in such regions. While it may have been a conscious political motivation for subsequent conquerors to knock down the temple walls of the vanquished and build their own churches on top, there likely were other unconscious causes as well.

As human beings, we detect the energy of our environments and those around us whether we realize it or not. We are drawn to where we receive a heightened sense of well-being. Power spots contain that energy naturally. When people also worship or open themselves in these places, it adds to the power and vibrates in the field. Vibrations are the property of space and timelessness into which we can all tap.

Certainty

I made my earliest trip to Palenque merely to have a holiday with friends. It wasn't then meant to be a spiritual undertaking. At that time, I had no knowledge of ancient Mayan history or traditions, but found myself attracted. Over the week that I was in the area I returned to the ruins several times, something continuing to draw me there.

One afternoon, I was sitting on a slight rise behind the palace, gazing at its perimeters. I suddenly became aware that I was seeing something in the air directly above the palace—colors. Thinking my vision was faulty, I looked away and glanced back. Unmistakable turquoise and terra cotta shimmered in the field around the building. What's more, when I turned to some of the temples, I saw the same thing. At the time, I filed this experience away as merely interesting and thought no more of it, other than as another slight curiosity.

The following year, I returned to the region with the same friends, a few added to make a small group, and plans to go again to the Palenque complex. But before going to that destination, we rented two bush planes and flew into the jungle to visit Yaxchilan and Bonampak, ruins not as accessible as Palenque. As I wandered around Bonampak, I entered a temple with a bas-relief scene unfolding on its wall and had the shock of my life. As opposed to the carved walls I had seen at Palenque, which had no color, color still remained in places in Bonampak—mostly turquoise and terra cotta! Not familiar with Mayan history, I'd had no knowledge that Palenque's temples and palace walls had also once all been painted. However, I saw evidence of that fact vibrating in the energy fields around the ruins in Palenque and right in front of my physical eyes there in Bonampak!

Once again, I could have decided these were merely curious experiences, if they had not led me to a certainty where I had previously only held a suspicion. All manifestations of what we call time vibrate in the ether and we have the ability to access them if we choose. Indeed, we may do so without even realizing it. It's based upon our resonance at any given time. These vibrations exist relative to any thought form, person or thing ever to have existed or to exist. This is true for the vibration that manifested as a man who became known as the Buddha and the one known as Hitler. All these vibrations exist. We choose which ones we will engage by virtue of our intent—or our intention. When we open to connecting with the Cosmos, we take on this very real possibility and probability.

Guidance

In my book *Calling Our Spirits Home* I relayed a dream that gave me both a warning and a prophecy. Eugene O'Neill appeared in the course of the dream metaphorically compelling me to write and advising that it would become part of my livelihood. It showed me essentially ignoring him and becoming distracted down another avenue. I had this dream well before I considered undertaking the book in question, or even any writing for that matter. I also knew very little about Eugene O'Neill and hadn't, in my memory, been exposed recently to anything he'd penned. Much later, when I finally decided to write, my attention was indeed split by a venture that proved, in the end, not only disappointing but also distinctly unprofitable. I hadn't been smart enough at the time to heed his advice.

Again, it's possible that this is just an interesting and coincidental story. But after I had started this present book and was finding all ways imaginable not to write—as writers sometimes do—Eugene O'Neill appeared to me again in a dream. This time it was very brief. But it was a flash I clearly recalled.

"I'll have to go," he said to me and began to turn away.

"Wait!" I cried out desperately, waking myself up.

After that I once again picked up my pen, so to speak. A few weeks later, I was cross-country visiting my parents. While there, I had dinner with an old friend. In the midst of our conversation, I told him about my unusual relationship with Eugene O'Neill. We laughed about it and went on to other topics.

When I returned to my parents' home late that night, they were already in bed. Being too energized by my hours long discussion with my friend, I looked for a way to unwind so that I could go to bed. Reading the newspaper is not a habit of mine. However, the newspaper was there and after scanning the front page, I opened it. There staring back at me was a photograph of Eugene O'Neill! In a column entitled "This Day in History," I was informed that on that date in 1946 "The Iceman Cometh" had opened on Broadway. I also noticed from the article that he had passed the year I was born. I may have been chuckling with my friend earlier that evening, but someone was having a big laugh at my expense then. It was a few more hours before I was able to retire for the night.

How is it that I could be the "protégé" of Eugene O'Neill? Or that simple events could arrange themselves in a way that I definitely glean meaning in them for my life? The only answer I have is that at those times when he actively manifested in my awareness, there must have been a resonance of some sort between us. If vibrations are similar, they often attract. I noticed that I saw him only when I was using delaying tactics, or was generally unconscious in my actions. Perhaps in his life, he knew those same patterns all too well. I can only feel deeply touched by his clipped, direct guidance and be grateful for it.

I haven't seen my mentor in a metaphysical manner in quite some time. But writing has become a regular practice for me. Maybe it's his intense dark eyes staring at me from the newspaper photo that I preserve on my desk that keeps me in line. He's had no further need to reappear.

My illustrations here lend a new meaning to possibility. If something has ever existed in some form, then it's still present on a certain level. In the instances above, I stumbled upon this truism. But we can consciously open to it. Holding the intent to connect with what would guide us, we can do so.

The Premise

Like an unconscious mantra held in the mind, we ask a question in any given moment. In asking the question, the answer naturally comes to us. Therefore, in holding the thought, *we ask the answer.* This is the paradox that guides our lives.

We cannot ask a question for which there is no answer. Our minds can't conceive of such. It is also true that what our minds cannot envision as reality, even though perhaps experienced, we wipe from conscious memory and reject, often trying to kill the messenger in the process. Through some fluke of determination when our minds can conceive of a wider reality, or at least have some inkling of acceptance, that conception will generate answers beyond the questions. This opening will then move us into new experiences through the wider framework of the mind—and we wonder how we got *there.*

This is not unlike driving on a highway, going into a trance state but continuing to drive, only to come later to the realization that many minutes have passed without conscious awareness. This is a common experience we've likely all had. We went "somewhere," but we didn't. Attention was merely shifted while what was automatic continued to perform.

There is nothing actually new in existence. What is has been and will always be. It is a fantasy to think anything will ever be totally obliterated. Even if we entertain the idea that some ancient scourge no longer exists, in fact it does. As long as one person gives attention to the scourge in question, that thought starts a process. It begins to create the possibility of attracting the vibration that then has the opportunity to segue into form. The more people who hold to the attraction, the more pull it has to materialize. This is how such mass tragedies as Hitler's Holocaust were able to occur.

It is equally true that as someone reaches out with questions of a higher vibratory nature and are joined by a number of others who do the same, we can create what seem like miracles to the ordinary mind. Hence, such manifestations of the Holy Virgin or other sacred figures in particular locales can be explained this way, as can long-distance healing of individuals through prayer circles. In truth, *all* these manifestations vibrate around us at any given moment.

It takes some sort of compatibility with the vibration, even if only wonder, to plug into it. This certainly explains how inventors can experience the "aha" that produces a discovery at the same time, when they may live across the world from each other. Then there may be an involvement of egos arguing that theirs was first, or there were spies involved. It's really that there was a likeness and strength of mutual intent of inquiry in the asking that brought the same vibration to all at the shared moments. It also demonstrates to me how I can often have what seem like extraordinary insights one day that I find validated in reading or experience the following day. It's the ensuing phenomenon of the foregoing meditation.

The aspect for us each to consider is not whether any of the aforementioned is true from the mind's perspective. It's more to notice the answers brought into our lives through the nature of the asking we each do unconsciously.

Begging the Question

In daily living, we mostly question, from habit, those things we think we already know. Indeed, since the mind portends we already know, the attraction is strong to be shown the same old answers—perpetually.

This is true because the mind loves to engage through the ego's desire to perpetuate itself. As discussed several chapters earlier, we create this unending cycle through the life beliefs we hold inside, whose asking answers the rut of our existence. It doesn't matter the nature of the rut, it's the burrow that feels familiar. Because we are such natural creatures of the routine, we are wont to give ourselves a leg up, at least until the rut becomes far worse than what we perceive is "out there."

There's a wonderful anecdote about Einstein. The story goes that a journalist invited Einstein to tell people the most important thing imaginable that would make a difference in their lives. Einstein said that he would instead ask them to answer a question.

"Is the world a friendly place?"

Depending how we each answer that question will frame the flavor of our lives. We will determine how safe we experience ourselves with others, and with the world in general. This will divulge the foundation we move from in fear, or in trust, at any given point. It has nothing to do with the fact that, indeed, there are events happening in the world that harm and people who harm, or that are joyful. By holding that question and answering it through our belief systems regarding safety, we attract to us what we believe will continue to fulfill us—even if it doesn't.

The bottom line is that we ceaselessly ask the answer—*how is this true?*—for whatever we hold in the ego's crusade.

Expanding the Framework

Since the mind wants to engage, which is its purpose, we need to work with what we have. We can use the mind in a way that allows us to go beyond what we have thus far been shown through the natural attraction of what is already resident there. The truth is that people who have chosen to devote themselves to the deeper life have made this distinction.

It stems first from the inner place of intent that stimulates an interior framework of inquiry outside the usual state. We can liken this inquiry to cinders placed underneath a mired wheel that provide enough traction for release from any previous entrapment. The beauty is that the Core Self already knows and owns Truth. But by allowing the queries to emerge from that space, the asking can create the experiences to inform the everyday self. Thus, we can collaborate with the very core aspect of ourselves to stretch the operating framework bit by bit—until unending galaxies become apparent.

Questions of the Quest

Using the *Re-membering Process* as a model, prior to the initial *Sparking*, we've been in a sleep state, experiencing varying levels of numbness in some or all parts of our lives. While it is possible to be aroused from the sleep, there's also the potential of remaining in the stupor of confusion, like a bear coming out of deep hibernation. Something needs to provide the leverage that will propel the awakening, for *the task of Sparking is waking up*. Holding these questions will begin to generate the raising of the head, the gazing of the eyes and the engaging of the body.

Where am I?
What am I feeling?
What am I lacking?

Once we are aware of what currently is, in order for the journey to evolve, we need to ascertain in what ways we have been untrue to the Core Self. In this way, we can determine what we need to detach ourselves from in order to create the space for something else to come to us. *The task of Separation is un-learning.* Therefore, we need to uncover how we might have learned to give our power away and how to take responsibility once more. The sometime painful answers

126

to these questions will give us the impetus, if we choose, to move *away from* a false past. We then will be shown the actual nature of our previous existence clearly.

> *Who am I not?*
> *How did I abdicate?*
> *How do I serve myself?*

Once we have this understanding, we can turn our attention to the *Search, whose task is widening possibilities.* To truly detach, we need to turn *toward* the chance of something else. Because this process is much like brainstorming that generates many choices, it can be a time of lighthearted play in the fields of opportunity. Allowing these questions to radiate will bring the potential right fit.

> *Who am I?*
> *What are the possibilities?*

If the journey is to continue, floating and trying on will eventually get old. The knowing of the Core Self is allowed to stand and reaches out to the everyday self. In the time of *Initiation, the task of assimilating* begins to ingrain the Truth. What was only held at the inner point will meet with the outer point. These questions will bring that meeting in the middle and create the opening to the next aspect of the process.

> *What are my gifts?*
> *Where am I going?*
> *What do I need?*

This circle brings us back to where we started and returning to the world, but with the Core Self risking exposure. *Re-entry requires the task of immersion.* It also requires discernment of what to show and how to re-engage in a sense, not because the Core Self cares about annihilation. That's not a possible occurrence anyway. It's more about what to show residents of a linear world about the beauty of the nonlinear domain in a way that they can create the *Sparking* for themselves. It's about being kindly patient with the fears of those who are elsewhere on the path, or still asleep to the dream they have been living. It's about finding the open framework within a structured society, and the tools of non-doing in their implementation through these points of departure.

> *How do I return?*
> *What gifts do I share?*
> *What is the structure?*
> *How do I implement?*

The way of a spiritual evolution that I call the *Re-membering Process* is through fully asking these answers. From there, we can extend our awe to enrapture even deeper experience and the wonder of All That Is.

Ultimately, it's about the willingness to engage no matter what— and being aware of the nature of what we are asking. It will surely come back to meet us along the way. The choice we all make is whether and when we take the lead.

CHAPTER ELEVEN

Living With Contrast

I had adjusted to the darkness. What had previously seemed so dark wasn't. There was enough light coming from a diminutive hole to the sky far above, as well as from the low entrance, that I was able to discern the other walls. Having circumambulated the small interior and groped my way into a corner, I was standing wedged, facing the center, my shoulders touching either wall for stability. I closed my eyes and moved into a meditative state.

Almost immediately, images swirled through my internal field, not stopping for me to identify the nature of them. Finally, with a backdrop like a fast-forwarded movie, stills were plucked out and pushed with intensity into the foreground to rest jarringly right in front of my inner eyes, as though demanding further study. They seemed to stay only long enough for my brain to register each image before that one disappeared and the next one arrived.

As sometimes happens when I receive images during trance states, these were parts from a larger whole, the wider aspect being invisible to me. But the pieces chosen to be revealed to me were crystal clear, strikingly so. The first one was filled solely with what appeared to be small widths of an ivory or oatmeal-colored cloth slightly overlapping one another. The next image had panned down and enlarged enough for me to realize that the cloth was wrapped over the head of a person. The face, from the eyebrows to chin, where the image concluded, was exposed. I somehow assumed it was male, but beyond that the face was nondescript to me.

Another shot showed the neck to its base uncovered, the shoulders and just below the collarbone shrouded. The picture halted there traveling no farther down the body, concentrating my gaze on the hollow of the throat. Suddenly, there was movement. The still became a movie. A hand moved into the picture holding what looked like a long quill. As I watched, the long fingers tightened their grip on the tube and forcefully punctured the soft U-shaped spot and held it there. I had the sense that something was being drawn out. While it may have been something physical that was removed, I had the understanding that it was the power contained therein that was ultimately meant to be captured. Then, the whole scene disappeared and I was once again aware of the ground beneath my feet and my shoulders against the walls.

I opened my eyes, stood for a few moments longer, looking around, realizing that I must have been connecting with one of those who had been buried in this *chullpa* at what we call death. I had an overwhelming desire to stay in this temple, this sanctified offering, but knew that it was time to go. I moved a few feet to my left, crouched and duck-walked through the place where the large square stone had been removed, into the bright afternoon light.

There I found my two traveling companions and Don Américo talking quietly, or just sitting. I joined them. After a while, Don Américo motioned, inviting us to follow him on a walk around the mesa's edge. I followed closely behind him, the others straggling farther back enjoying the view. After a distance, he came to a sudden halt and brought me over to the very rim and gestured to a flat rock jutting out below, indicating I was to light there and meditate.

I balked, clearly telling him with *my* gesture, "I don't think so!"

After all, he had no way of knowing—or perhaps he did—about the phobia of heights that I'd had for a long period in my life. I'd undergone a process some years before that released the fear, but I wasn't sure I wanted to test it to the extent to which he was directing me.

"Yes!" he said to me adamantly in Spanish. "This is good for your work."

Figuring he knew how to hook me, and grumbling a bit internally to myself, I acquiesced. Don Américo went on about his own business, leaving me to find the way to my perch. I didn't want to think about the sheer drop of at least a thousand feet and preferred to look instead at the narrow ground where I would place my feet. I charted a short course and then carefully picked my way to the stone and settled into a comfortable seated position. Legs crossed, spine straight and ready to meditate, a bizarre urge ran through me. There was a strong part of me that wanted nothing more than to physically leap into the lonely, empty space in front of me that stretched for miles! Quickly quelling that impulse and pushing it from my mind, I closed my eyes.

The stillness that had begun in the *chullpa* made itself known again and I immersed myself in the quiet. After a while, I heard a tranquil wind from the right, whistling softly, slowly coming along the perimeter of the mesa. Surprisingly, I felt it touch my body and instead of moving around me, it went through me on its way to the left. The wind was immensely long, its blowing gentle, but when its tail finally exited, it left me bodiless, having indulgently thrown me into the abyss I'd wished for after all. I dissipated into the dark nothingness of the Void while, at the same time, I merged with the totality of the landscape, covering it. The silence was such that I have no words for it, but a feeling of profound tranquility and yet expansive joy permeated the being that I call myself.

I have no idea how long I remained in that state, a minute or an hour. It was timeless. Somewhere in the midst of it, something compelled me to open my eyes, and I received a jolt. Not only was my consciousness not fully in my body—so to speak—when I did so, but I had also erased my awareness that I was seated on the precipice of a very high mesa rather than the usual ground! In addition, I had catapulted myself from the blackest black into the brilliant light of the high Andean sun. I slammed my eyes shut, unwilling to experience the colossal contrast.

Slowly though, I began to feel the outlines of my body and the friendly stone supporting me. This time I took my time raising my outer eyelids and gazed without fear across the miles of the *Altiplano*, the high plains, all the way to the ring of mountains on the other side. I found that I was taken with the beauty of this place that many would consider barren and lifeless. I had discovered the richness hidden from casual eyes.

Bi-locating

While my compulsion to jump into thin air was unexpected at the time, I've experienced it before in high places. After having talked with others, I realize that I'm not alone. This is a common urge. What I've come to understand is that it's a petition from the deepest part of us. It's the soul's sense of wanting freedom. It's a strong inner existential yearning that calls for merging rather than separation. Being in the body and mind we experience ourselves as a unit, separated from all else by the skin we wear. We've forgotten that we are everything else as well. It's a wisdom most have lost. We've segmented life into either/or.

Perhaps that was the potency that I saw extracted in my vision of the mummy in the *chullpa*. Only those considered powerful, such as elder priests and nobility, were purported to be interred in these towers. Particularly sorcerers or shamans know how to blend, and charismatic leaders possess the ability to effectively transition even whole nations.

I've often wondered about suicide. Usually we think of people who've made that choice as doing so because their lives were horrendously painful in some way. Are there ever those who consciously choose this method of annihilation because they can no longer stand separation from the greater Unity? Knowing no other way to experience merging, they put an end to their lives on this plane.

In his books, Carlos Castenada gave examples of sorcerers leaping over a mountain's edge, or some other void, and turning up safely elsewhere. In esoteric literature, we may find documentation of mystics bi-locating, being seen in two different geographical places at once. While these practices are probably not on the list of skills to learn for most of us, if we are to deepen our path we need to at least learn metaphorically how to intermingle non-ordinary and ordinary reality freely.

In the course of discovering how to shift easily between realities, or ultimately be in both at once, we first experience increasingly intense contrast between the two. This is natural and we undergo it in a variety of ways.

Silence

How is it possible to describe the great silence that prevails when we move beyond the mind and body? Any attempt at words wouldn't do that reality justice. And yet, there is such sweetness, a profound resting place. The heart intuitively knows that it has finally found its home. Separation is over. Merging has occurred. Unity is realized.

As though a curtain is drawn open to admit the sunlight, we discover that the Truth for which we've strived is revealed to be ever-present. We merely partitioned it off. If we've chosen to fully immerse ourselves, without fear, into the effervescent warmth of nothingness, we automatically want to remain there. The everyday world matters little in this flow. We sense that we can ride this wave into eternity. And we do.

But with the exception of very few seasoned travelers, the body-mind and pull of the ordinary world segment reality and draw our attention back to the place where we usually reside. The transition isn't necessarily an easy one unless we've traversed it many times and grown used to the departure and return, instead living in the interplay of the overlap. Then it becomes seamless. Until then, we have differentiation. With differentiation we may have paramount awareness of uncomfortable contrast.

Emerging from silent nothingness, returning to the physical plane would perhaps best be gently nurtured. Ideally, we would leave and reappear in a natural setting to the lilt of a birdsong; musically ushering us back through the doorway, settling us kindly into the seat of everyday reality.

But we rarely have the choice. While I have noticed that I am most prone to experience these states while in nature, I cannot orchestrate them. They occur spontaneously. Nor can I hold onto them should I decide to try to do so. While I have not yet carried the great silence with me permanently upon the shift and refocus to my day-to-day life, its merging has sometimes endured for some good lengths, enough for me to know without a doubt what is possible. And the shimmer of that possibility remains ensconced in the cocoon of my being.

Moving toward that eventual point, there are glimpses, small teases. There's also another aspect to these favors. If we're going to travel the deeper path, we need to learn how to navigate it. If we were thrown into such a sea without any tools we would be seriously disadvantaged at best. So, there are the continuing series of re-entries we make to increase our awareness of the geography. If we pass back and forth over similar area enough times, perhaps we will become familiar enough with the territory to make the one transparent to the other. In the meantime, the transitions can be shocking until we recognize them for what they are.

Coming from the great silence, we are still initially immersed in it upon the return. And the external voice with which we speak has been drowned in its vastness. The brain doesn't operate to send the signals required to activate it. Nor do we normally want to do so. The silence is so complete that to move from it has been literally painful in my experience. Any sounds other than most of those associated with nature, or some forms of music, have a similar effect to sticking one's finger into an electrical socket. Others' voices, of any timbre, can be like fingernails scraping across a blackboard, or a dentist's drill. Car motors revving and issuances from a television feel like a violent physical assault. It can actually be likened to a person who has been stone deaf, but begins, through some intervention, to hear. The majority of sound is then raucous, feeling like an affront to the soul.

For myself, there is a reluctance to engage in any usual interaction with others at these times. This is so for a few reasons. Unless we are just content to share the silence and allow it to carry the deeper correspondence, I'm often unable to communicate any other way. While I am able to see and hear amply indeed, my mind is still "impaired," needing much time to swim legions up out of some depth, with my voice in tow, to be able to pop words out into space. Attempting too soon, I would resemble a fish opening and closing its mouth, discharging nothing of much sense.

Just so, if I am with those who are willing to be companions in stillness, what each of us experiences individually is only amped exponentially through the power of the circle.

Another reason for my own quiet is that I find that the minute I start to speak, I begin to dissipate the energy which I naturally want to retain as long as possible. That's different, however, than speaking or teaching from an infused state. In this case, there's no mistaking the command of higher consciousness spontaneously moving through to transmit to those who are open to listening. The voice has purpose.

In the former, it's the contained caress of silence that finally imbues the latter voice through experiential knowledge that must be held long enough to inform the verbalizing. Speaking too soon then doesn't allow the gelling to happen, letting the real cellular knowledge seep away. What can return in force is the conflagration of the habitual mind trying to overwhelm Truth. In the conflict, Truth may seem to slide just out of sight, even though it's always within reach.

The silence may come when we make a space, take time out from normal activities. It can come through meditation, using the breath to empty the mind; finally inspiring the no-breath. It can come through a walk in the forest, mindfully, slowly placing the feet firmly on the earth, connecting in such a way that the body is no longer a body, but a bubble of energy skimming along the surface of life. It can come through intentfully opening the crown center of the head during times of creative expression. We only know that silence has visited when we return to our work later and wonder who has written the passages or painted an image nowhere in our memory to have done so. But oftentimes, no matter how we prepare the ground, it doesn't come. At least not to the depth we would choose, or the habitual voice imposes instead.

And sometimes it can come unbeckoned at most inconvenient moments! Several years ago, a friend and I were going to lunch at a busy restaurant. I had just slid into the booth when I suddenly seemed to be beside myself. While I could still see, I was aware of nothing else except what I can only describe as a solid column of energy descending through my crown, so powerful it removed me from my body, along with any thoughts I may have had in my mind. I could only look at my friend as he kept asking, "Are you okay?" Solely after the silence allowed me to finally sidle back to join my body-mind could I answer at all. It was a good hour before I fully felt like my "self" again.

At the time, I put the incident on the much longer than normal durations I had been spending in meditation seeking clarity and balance due to some difficulties I was undergoing. But still today these charges come periodically, through the Crown Chakra or Third Eye, momentarily transmitting the energy of the great silence, verging on the loss of body-mind awareness, honing my abilities to continue daily actions nonetheless.

Alien Life Forms

In the movie *Windtalkers*, which used as its base the *Diné*, or Navajo, code talkers during World War II, there was a scene I will long remember. Two of the main characters, destined to be code talkers, had just arrived in boot camp. They'd already had a few less than respectful interactions with non-*Diné* as they were trying to get acclimated. At each of the exchanges, the *Diné* recruits would exhibit looks of shock or bewilderment at the brusque responses they received. They finally came to stand together in the midst of others who were moving hurriedly along like ants on the way to meet their fate. One said to the other, "I've never seen so many white people." The message that clearly came across was that there was a vast difference in code, one the new talkers would be wise to break in order to get along in that environment.

The distinction between the experiences of the two characters in the film and most of those who have passed certain milestones in the context of the spiritual journey is that we know the code that perplexes them only too well. That's why we chose to step on the path less taken in the first place.

But there comes a time when we've become transfixed with a certain kind of amnesia. The code with which we were previously so familiar becomes absolutely bizarre to us. What was once the norm is no longer. Something else has taken its place.

A threshold has been crossed. While the preempting process may have been gradual, there is suddenly a point that comes when the crossing is complete. At that point, we look back over the bridge and can no longer relate to the place we left. It appears to be a nowhere land. The code we used to live is so much gibberish to us.

We often experience increasing chasms between others and ourselves. That is, unless those others have been traveling in lockstep with us and passed through similar terrain. With the gap, we may suddenly find ourselves strangers in formerly well-known territory. Or depending on our tendencies, we may decide that our previous peers are the ones who are alien life forms.

The feeling of alienation is common. But what is true is that no matter how foreign we feel, there will be those with whom we are comfortable. Like is attracted to like and we can discover community and support in *whatever* realm we deem valid. It is also the case that the farther we move from mainstream thought, the fewer we will find to form a consortium. The folk that we do discover will then often gather to shape what seems like a thirsty oasis in an otherwise parched desert.

There is a fact concerning the quality of vibration we emit depending on the focus we individually have. If we choose to stew in any of our historical limitations, there is an emotional heaviness that slows our energy frequencies down. As we concentrate instead on the jewels of the Core Self, our literal being is lighter and our vibration speeds up. It's this factor, matching and mismatching energies, to which we respond when we experience camaraderie or estrangement.

Also know that there isn't anything inherently "bad" about where many people continue to be, or where we ourselves once were. It's merely a reflection of level of awareness, wider choices, and discernment of long-term ramifications. As we unceasingly make the decisions to further our commitment toward the authentic life, we will walk the land that automatically leads us from one bridge to yet others. In the country in-between there will always be a new code to learn. The newly acquired language will have its own secrets that we will eventually forget as well.

What Awaits

There's a shared experience that we've all had at different points. It matters little whether we've been to a formal retreat, engaged in a week of camping at a primitive site or merely carved out some days to lie on a beach or travel cross-country. We step outside everyday time and create a cocoon. An enclosure surrounds us, normally inhibiting worries to the degree that they go underground for a while.

I was once astounded at the finesse with which a friend of mine did this very thing as we prepared to take a trip together. He arrived at my home the day prior to our departure with great anxiety weighing him down. Due to some unpleasant circumstances his entire livelihood was heading into a mudslide. As we set off the next day, I marveled at how he seemed to set the concerns completely aside for the duration of our foray. By doing so, he created a space that allowed some clarity to emerge. He returned home with a new outlook and some potential solutions.

It can also happen that during retreat times we open, trying on new perspectives and behaviors. Juxtaposed to that beauty, whatever is resident within us that could barricade the bridge will usually come up and out, sometimes with a vengeance! These occurrences can be disturbing to the individual, but also stunning to fellow travelers or retreatants, coming like a jolt out of the blue during otherwise wonderful occasions.

If we are recipients of a projectile from someone else and have a response—beyond surprise—then we know that we, too, have something to learn through the incident. If instead we merely witness the event, we can be assured the missile hasn't found fertile ground within us. We can then send silent support, through our non-response, that the person will work through the internal challenges.

Sometimes, though, all is sensational in our cocooning and it's only upon our literal return to the everyday life that things seem to go wrong. The castigating internal voice that was magically hushed during our sojourn reinstates itself louder than ever. Activities are blocked. Bliss slips away. Frustration takes its place. Whatever seeks to hold us back will attempt to do so, encouraging the opportunity to forget the cocoon. Instead of emerging as a butterfly, we regress to the larva!

How we handle any exacerbation of limitations that have contained us in the past is a sure measure in the course of our opening process. It is expressly our abilities to remain aware and modulate the release of the old habits through rapt attention and intent that ensures the ever-deepening cycles of the Re-membering Process. We then ultimately transition into the land of no contrast. And all is fluid.

In NLP, Neuro-Linguistic Programming, there is a change process called "Foreground/Background" that lessens, or potentially obliterates, physical pain or mental irritations that a person may have. A practitioner explores with the sufferer the internal structure of what they are enduring. As an example, this survey may include bodily felt sensations, internal dialogue, imagery and so on. The practitioner then finds something that is similar in the person's experience, but to which they have either a neutral or positive response. In the case of a chronically painful joint, a counterexample might be another joint that is flexible. Or with sensitivity to the sound of a person's voice, another person's voice may be used.

While the two explore the structure of the analogous context, the practitioner suddenly directs the person's attention to something that would be common to both settings, "Are you aware of the tip of your nose?" While anchoring the complainant's attention on the innocuous, out-of-awareness aspect, the practitioner quickly diverts the person's notice back to the original point of contention. But mysteriously, the discomfort is no longer there, or is greatly decreased. The former sufferer is baffled, the mind confused, but lightened considerably. The practitioner is invariably delighted.

140

It seems as though this kind of negotiation also occurs when the great silence permeates. We know through scientific research the very small percentage of the brain we exercise. I sense that within the remainder resides the entry point to the great silence. What is a common experience to both is respiration. The secret of our deliverance was hidden from us when the term Holy Ghost was mistranslated in the Bible. The Source was resident in the accurate translation Holy Breath.

In meditation practice I sometimes ask people to choose some problematic little nut they are wanting to release, but has a way of remaining. Then, with the inspiration coming from the silent mind, we caress the stubborn thought form with our breath. And on the exhalation we begin to shrink the size of it through a natural relaxation. With each subsequent inhalation the silent mind automatically comes more to the foreground, while the troubling aspect moves to the background and often dissipates altogether. We find that we have this choice in attention. We can realize that Divinity is providing us with ongoing resuscitation, which is not separate from ourselves. We decide the mere shift in concentration. We can choose what then brings us to the enduring conduit finalizing Holy Birth.

The Trick of Light

In the Southwest, the ponderosas and pinons have been dying by the millions. First stressed by drought, bark beetles, then scale have been able to gain a more than ample foothold. What was an ongoing natural process to clear the forests and send the weakened back to the earth to be composted has become what seems to some like an inordinate chance for nasty little invaders to devastate the beauty of our natural resources. There exists a communal sorrow for most human inhabitants around these areas as we witness something acting well beyond our control removing what we value.

On the eve of the United States and British invasion of Iraq, just upon dusk and the hour of power, I was driving home, winding through the forest climbing slightly in elevation, my heart heavy. As I came up a rise, I expected to see the usual huge swathes of rusty brown fire sticks amidst the otherwise dark green of the forested mountains a short distance away. What I saw instead took my breath away and caused me to slow to a snail's pace to engage with the sight for as long as possible.

The seemingly decimated trees were glowing with an unearthly orange-red light of such an intense saturation of the like that I'd only seen once before, almost appearing to leap out of the landscape.

Now, logic says that it was sunset. The sun had just descended behind the mountain to the west and this trick of light was merely a reflection of rays striking the dead trees. Indeed, this was my second response—after the one of awe. But I believe that the overwhelming reverence I first recorded was the correct reaction, because something else pointed my notice toward the other trees. Those trees were wearing their usual colors. No intensity there. Nor did the few clouds in the sky carry any more sunset brilliance than normal.

The sole time I'd witnessed a previous showing of this kind was a deeply spiritual event. Like a dealer displaying his hand under unlikely circumstances, I sense that the power of Creation was purposefully revealed to me. The message was clear in both cases. What seems devastating is not. What seems hidden is not. What we bring to light will change our perspective. From the farther reaches of the Cosmos, all is still as all is fluid.

CHAPTER TWELVE

Thresholds

"Zorro?" Don Américo inquired of a passerby. The man said a few sentences in Quechua, gesturing in such a way that I realized we were to go over a few streets.

We were in Paucartambo, a place barely large enough to be called a town. We had paused on the way to Salk'a Wasi, Don Américo's ancestral home located several hours outside Cusco. We still had at least an hour to go, depending on the conditions of the road, or as he had already intimated, if the mountain hadn't "fallen down." Having already experienced the circumstances of the route we had thus far driven, and knowing from previous trips it would not at all improve, I was happy to put my feet on the ground for a while and stretch my legs.

We were interested in masks. Paucartambo was known for the Festival of the Virgin of Carmen. Each July, thousands of Indians descend upon this small burg where no conventional lodging exists, to find shelter somewhere in order to take part in the traditional dances whose origins stretch back centuries to the times when Catholicism was introduced. Over countless years, the celebration had become a syncretistic diversion from an often difficult existence for those who live in the mountains.

A dancer isn't complete without a mask, signifying a particular persona out of the many folkloric characters. Indeed, in the days after the conquistadors came to Peru, donning a mask was one of the few ways the *brujas* and *pacos*, sorcerers and medicine women and men, could come out of isolation, mix with their people and have some measure of protection against being tortured and killed.

Local artisans labor the entire year to produce enough masks to satisfy the demand during the festivities. Even though it was February, we hoped to find a good selection from which to choose some souvenirs.

When Don Américo indicated we should track down Zorro because he was the best, I thought he was kidding. I had in my mind the hero of the old radio and movie shows.

After wandering the cobble-stoned streets some more without luck, and being redirected by townspeople a few times, we came to what could hardly be described as a storefront. It had no windows and its doors were closed. Not to be deterred, Don Américo called something in Quechua over the tall iron fence connected to the dilapidated building. Presently, we heard a man's voice answering, apparently telling us he would come open the door. Don Américo raised his index finger, signaling we should wait, and said quietly, "They call him 'The Fox.'"

I heard sounds from inside of things being moved and the door unlocked. The translation made sense, but I was still curious how someone would garner such a name. The answer came when the door swung open and the artist appeared to greet us. Unusual looking for a Peruvian, his hair was fox red and as bristly as a hedgehog's, standing straight up from his head. He also had a level of intensity to his demeanor that he'd likely worn for years. Don Américo and Zorro greeted each other like lost friends. We were invited inside and entered a small, ill-lit room with cracked mud walls. I could see the light of the courtyard beyond through another door.

It was like entering Gepetto's workshop. Pinocchio wasn't hang-ing around, but I didn't miss him. Low, narrow shelves lined the perimeter walls. Hooks were placed sporadically on the higher places. Papier-mâché masks in various stages of completion either hung or sat in the spaces provided for them.

There was a white, narrow-faced one with black eyebrows in an attitude of surprise and pursed lips. I could almost hear the "Oh!" it silently expelled. There was a black-faced one with round, apple cheeks, merry, laughing eyes and a gold goatee. In all the various characters, my favorite was the billy goat with real chin hairs and a serpent uncurling itself from a horn and wiggling down his forehead. There were a few that had dark, demonic qualities as well. We had a good time choosing some to take with us and bartering for them as the custom dictated.

Having completed our purchases, we left Paucartambo and continued on our way. Don Américo had been quiet for a while, as though he was reflecting on something. He finally spoke and told a story.

For many years, Zorro had a problem with drink. And as universally happens with such issues, it had negative effects. He wasn't a happy reveler, but a morose loner whose life was spiraling out of control. He became obsessed with mask making. But it wasn't just any of the masks that entrapped him. It was the demonic ones. Perhaps seeing his own tortured soul reflected in the images he made, he was gripped by this activity. He couldn't tear himself away. The compulsion to recreate his own hell sucked him into timeless places. Every waking moment, deep into the night, he worked. And as he did so, he began to lose touch with everyday reality. Days and nights were a continuum of his fingers working, almost as if they were under someone else's command, transmuting malignant spirits from thought form into material existence. Finally, he teetered on the precipice of what appeared to be psychosis. Then the many faces of his doppelgänger escorted him through a portal into another world. And something of a profound nature happened there.

When he returned, he was vague when attempting to relay the experience to others. There were no words for such. Nor could he say where the place was exactly. But he was very clear that the catalytic event occurred. And it changed him exponentially. His obsession for demonic mask making ceased. He no longer had a problem with drink. A normal life emerged. But it was more meaningful in the living of it.

Escort Service

Zorro went through a threshold. Whether with paranormal accompaniment or through stealthy tricks of the mind, his fixation became so grand that it could no longer be contained. The bubble popped. And he was ushered into another dimension, another reality. This was literally so because, when he was reintroduced into this plane, the flavor of his old reality was gone. He had experienced transformation.

As any of us move from one phase of the Re-membering Process to another, or one Dwelling Place to another, we may go through a series of dark nights. Some are mere disturbances of "sleep." Some are what seem to be unending, full-blown nightmares.

In order to loosen our handshake with a thought form or habit that doesn't serve us, we often inhabit every corner of it; revisit every subtlety, in order to finally be repelled by it. We delve deeply into the form of our own particular ways of abdication.

When we focus on something intensely, we give it power. The obsession looms larger and attracts its fulfillment. When it becomes so concentrated that we can hardly stand it, some of us pull back and store it away. The convolution submerges. It goes underground—for a while—until it raises its head to be considered again. Thus cycles the request for authenticity.

Others have a tolerance for such heat that when the delusion is most grandiose they increase it still. And finally the pressure blows and its immensity propels them through a worm hole, turning them inside out, the force shearing any last vestiges of the old reality from their grasp. They are brought painfully to their knees and then taught, through divine means, to stand again.

This is the path of purification. Those of us who are dedicated to becoming clean and clear, to being absolutely present to All That Is, will follow it relentlessly. We will do so until we finally release whatever form of fear has held us tethered in place. And then we will continue undeterred—knowing there is even more necessary.

The severity of this evolution will depend on the degree of clinging to disillusion we practice and our own penchant for drama. Even so, as we get closer to those inner Dwelling Places, to the real Initiation, the dark nights are perhaps more full-blown. A complete embrace with the Divine is so close and we are vigorously urged to lose the veil—to pull it away and see what remains, if anything at all of previous experience.

Subterfuge

In the process, the ego mind will throw up any number of obstructions in on-going attempts to block the way. Yet, these are the very things that can open us and we can attune through them. It's a matter of recognition.

Unfortunately for me, I more often became aware of the lesson after the fact. It takes acute observation and fine-tuning of the Witness to catch yourself at your own foolishness. But then we wouldn't have the opportunity for refinement if there hadn't been a time when we were clueless. It is this understanding that can allow us to make peace with the past—and not repeat at least that particular aspect of it.

My folly was huge. I didn't recognize it until two years after its completion and I had spent a little time with someone who had played a major part in it. After the visit, on the daylong drive home through mountainous desert, I had entered a state of mindlessness, a kind of reverence for the landscape. When I had rested there long enough, my vehicle automatically guiding itself, little bubbles of truth began to arise from the still point inside. And when reality had coalesced enough, it finally merged with the terrain to the degree that all was laid out for me to see.

I had a panoramic view of a stream that had run through past events, its course muddying and eroding what was fertile land. Disparate waters do often intertwine and create even more force, can clarify the causeway, but the gestalt that generated then was relative to me taking full responsibility for my part in the parody.

Rather than whipping myself, I felt immense relief and was truly amazed at the complexity in which the process had played itself out. I also felt grateful that I had engaged with such a person, whose very nature would ensure an intense roller coaster ride, would induce greatly repressed responses in me and would produce such a guaranteed continuum of climactic occurrences that I could not deny the threshold through which I was ultimately catapulted.

The content of our considerable drama is of little importance. The elements of my own folly are where I find significance. Through them, my life and consciousness took a turn of consequence.

It had taken a journey of many years, one through ignorance, to doubt, and then consistent convincing for me to finally accept the gift of intuition that I had been given. At that point, I embraced it fully. As I did so, it got stronger. I had visions and bodily felt sensations guiding me that I trusted absolutely. Sometimes auditory messages would come. I made decisions and acted through these signals. My life was richer and even took on what seemed, from the perspective of others, to be a magical quality and every now and then a foolhardy one. For me, I found great comfort in recognition of the birthright we all are given. Thus the Divine supports us.

Unknowingly, there were also other ways I was being nurtured. The nurturance was through learning what was still resident in me that would tarnish or misdirect any guidance that came. I had keen clarity regarding the path my life would take and a strong sense of who would travel beside me. While I steadily followed my sixth sense, I also put a caveat on its intelligence—expectation. I began to place all kinds of parameters on the final destination; *exactly* what it would look like, sound like, feel like. And over the next couple of years I proceeded to push tenaciously toward fulfilling the tight little box into which I had contained my dream.

When we push, we are often met with its complement. Force begets force. People and events don't necessarily like to be controlled in such ways. As things increasingly didn't come to fruition in expressly the way I deemed, not at all, or just the opposite, my disappointment and frustration increased. Things began to fall apart, to unravel. And then I recognized at a profound level that I had *no* control. I had colluded with illusion.

A bit later in this particular leg of the unfolding, I had a metaphysical experience whereby what I saw with my eyes vacated, cone by cone, until I was left with nothingness. The veil had been removed. Nothing of recognition remained. What I thought was "reality" didn't even exist. None of it was real. I remember a thought flitting across my mind at that point, "I know how people go crazy."

When the mind finally admits to illusion, we cannot handle it at an ego level because, in that instant, the ego realizes that it doesn't endure. This experiential knowledge threw me into an abyss. I entered my own dark night.

What I thought had been my foundation, the illusory one, crumbled. My understanding at that time was that I had placed all my trust on intuition, a trust that had been years in the confirming.

I believed I had been misguided. My faith had been betrayed. My internal world and its outer manifestations fell apart. Someone who knew me had asked how I was doing, seeing the difficulty in my life. I'd answered, "I'm trying to figure out who I am." It was as though the statement had come from far away. It seemed that I hadn't spoken it.

Indeed, I was in search of my Self. My identity was gone. I felt as though I was wandering in some desert in search of an oasis. But the mirage kept on disappearing as I would get close to it. Did it look like psychosis? I doubt it. However, from a narrow clinical standpoint, I was having many of the symptoms—regular auditory and visual "hallucinations" and other manifestations.

Was I teetering on some razor's edge? Absolutely. My knees were weak and shaky. And even though all around me was uncertain, and downright frightening, there was the still point that held me steady at a core level through all of it. It was this enduring aspect of my Core Self that persistently created the thrust that would drive me to that edge and then, finally, create a calm that allowed me to step through the farther doorway. I had already been through the free fall and bottomed out.

The move through that specific threshold generated over time and culminated with my drive through the desert two years later. It happened well after the dust had settled around the precipitating events and I had regained a sense of stability. That time I hadn't been in angst searching out some mirage, but in a state of appreciation for the evolving topography. And the truth came. The foundation that had cracked had been the need to tightly control. In that moment, I could see that intuition was the expectancy that intent generated. I need only follow the cues given to me in my daily life, through synchronicities, to its fulfillment. It was not intent that had betrayed me, but my own very limited intention that had caused my derailment. I was ecstatic for the fierce magnificence of the journey.

We all have follies, messages we give ourselves about "not being enough" or its polar opposite regarding "entitlement." Perhaps it's about feeling helpless, hopeless or unsafe. We can guarantee that the people and events will show up in our lives to ensure our notice of the lies we tell ourselves. We just need to sort through and acknowledge the falsehoods.

Fixate on them. Dip into all their subtleties. Give them power. Create the intensity. Then let these follies be your escort. Attune to them in such a way that they can usher you through a threshold to another dimension—the nowhere of freedom.

And then look back. Witness the ludicrousness of the gyrations through which you put yourself. Finally, have compassion and gentle humor toward the fool within.

Secret Initiations

There are things we aren't told. If we search for the key to the secrets, they're mostly hidden. When we do come across some clues, they may make interesting or intriguing knowledge. But ultimately the entry into understanding is through exposure. We generally don't even begin to look for this brand of education until we've begun to touch the edges of it experientially and have questions. It doesn't come bidden, but unbidden, through openings we create. However, there's no formula to generate the opening. When we've been seasoned a little, more usually begins to come. And even then, there's still Mystery.

There are metaphysical and paranormal episodes I've alluded to throughout this book. I'll now describe some of those things clearly as they happened in my experience. This is not for sensational content, but to record these events with the intent of letting others know the nature of what can occur. It doesn't mean that it will, as everyone is different. However, I found great solace when I finally discovered fleeting references in spiritual, and even some psycho-spiritual literature to the types of things that sometimes manifest at certain points on the path. It verified for me that I wasn't a lunatic, just deeply engrained in the awakening of consciousness.

While I have been a practitioner of meditation for well over twenty years, during the time when my foundation was dissolving beneath me, I began to do it more intensively. I would meditate for up to four or five hours at different periods during the day or night. Feeling my reality slipping away, I was attempting to hold onto some level of normalcy and calm. I knew meditation to perform those functions for me and, additionally, often produced insights into my own condition.

I began to have more visions during meditation, but not just any old images. I would see pieces of a robe made out of coarse material, sandaled, dusty feet and such. Strangely, I *knew* that these were parts being shown to me, the whole being Jesus. I felt this was unusual for me in particular since I wasn't raised in an organized religion. In fact, I'd had little subjection at all except what we're all exposed to at least peripherally in our culture. I'd had no prior relationship with Jesus of Nazareth or the Christ Consciousness, nor was I specifically seeking one out. Yet, there He was and continued to be. Once during a meditation, He reached out and touched me with oil at the Third Eye. I literally felt the annointing. Another time, I saw His robed arm with a finger pointing toward a line of people walking in a line away from us, bundles on their backs, as though I was being directed to join them, perhaps being told it wasn't time to jump off the edge on which I was poised.

The climactic point in this period though was finally when, one morning, I was experiencing such mental angst that I was actually crying out for help and nearly tearing my hair from my head. I somehow surrendered my anguish. And then I saw a hazy figure appear on my right, audibly saying to me, with the gentlest voice imaginable, "Don't be troubled, my child." I sensed the top of my head being lightly stroked.

The supreme compassion I heard in His voice and the warmth I felt from His hand caused me to break down and weep, a real gusher. I cried out all my sorrow, loss and fear. And when I was finally dry, I sat there cross-legged on the floor for the longest time. Then I got up and went into my bedroom to dress. Emerging, the entire house was filled with the strong, sweet smell of blossoms. My deep suffering had gone. My life began to seem more solid. I felt safe. Things began to turn around for me after that.

I haven't had quite those images or heard His voice so clearly since that time. But I periodically feel His undeniable presence. And sometimes when I'm with someone and we're doing healing work, I smell blossoms still.

It was also during this time of concentrated meditation, that I began to have a sound in my ears—continually. It's always there if I choose to notice it. It's here with me now as I write these words. It's a kind of tone. It's never unpleasant and sometimes can even change into a kind of faint chirping, almost a singing. From the beginning, I never thought it was tinnitus. I somehow recognized it as the sound of Creation. And sometimes when I'm in retreat with others we share in the hearing of it. These are times when we're all in an altered state, beyond what is considered the norm. My understanding is that when I was engaged in that period of deep, ongoing meditative practices, I broke through some barrier. I no longer do hours long meditation as a usual course, but a shorter one still starts every day. However, the effects of those times, and its reinforcements, are now an integral part of who I am.

There is another phenomenon that I find unusual, my sense of smell. Under everyday circumstances, I have a poor sense of smell. An odor has to be strong for me to notice it. But if it comes from a paranormal or otherworldly source, my abilities turn keen. In this book, I've already mentioned scenting tobacco during times of meditation and otherwise. I recognize it as a ceremonial accoutrement, probably from one line of my ancestry. In my previous book, *Calling Our Spirits Home*, I wrote about a long encounter I had with a discarnate spirit who would announce his presence through a putrid smell.

This capability regarding smell showed up long before I recognized the sources generating it. Years ago, I lived in an old house built in the 1920s. It had a mudroom off the kitchen with a separate entrance. A previous owner had turned it into a half-bath and barred the outside door. One day I had been out for a while and returned. I went into the old mudroom. When I did, I smelled the strong, stinky odor of cigars! I certainly didn't smoke them and none of my friends did either. I was alarmed and thought my home had been violated by a break-in. However, when I went back into the kitchen, a few feet away, there was no smell. When I re-entered the mudroom, the wisps were there, albeit a little weaker. This occurrence remained a mystery until later when these things began to happen occasionally. Then I realized that some previous resident, one who had transitioned, had been paying his old home a visit.

On the spiritual path, there are also effects created through the subtle energy field we each have and whatever forces may drive them. In the beginning, after I had been regularly meditating for a fairly short period of time, I had what I can only describe as energy bubbles that must have been bumping up against some blockages. They became more acute over time and caused my body to seem, to me, as though it was being pulled over, almost folding itself in half to my right side. I asked someone to observe me one time when I was experiencing this phenomenon. The person told me my body

154

had remained upright. After a long while, this pressure disappeared. The blockages must have opened.

Over time my sensitivity toward feeling my own energy and that of others has increased dramatically. In the process, there have been phases through which I've been that, upon their completion, seem to further expand my capacity for energetic awareness and spiritual fortitude.

When I was engaging in the intensive meditative practices mentioned earlier, I started having nausea. It wouldn't happen during the actual practice, but would appear, out of nowhere, periodically during the day. I wasn't ill in any way that could cause it. It would stay for usually no longer than thirty minutes, often less, and then leave. It didn't incapacitate me. It was just there. The sporadic nausea lasted for about one month and hasn't returned.

A few years later, I went through a period when I would awaken in the night around 3 a.m. to violent energy rushes. They would start at my feet and would ascend to my head in forceful waves. It felt like I was being ravished. It was well beyond my control to stop. It was terrifying at first. But I quickly realized it was a passage of some sort and gave over to it. My guess is that it was a kundalini opening. I got very little sleep during that time, but was able to maintain just fine during the day. These happenings ceased after about six weeks and have not returned.

What took its place for a long time was what I can relate as a very subtle shimmering movement of energy that originated right below the navel at the Sacral Chakra and dissipated by the time it reaches my Heart Chakra. It's strongest near the Solar Plexus and has a pleasurable, erotic quality to it. It was present frequently every day and has lessened over a nearly three-year timeframe. It still calls on me occasionally.

While the aforementioned forms are what we may imagine would be part of the path, and some of them we even hope for, there was another form with which I began to have experience that was explicitly unwelcome. I learned that I could not deny that the dark side exists as well—and sometimes visits.

In an earlier time, I had felt some kind of presence pressing down on me at night every now and again. I began to smell something musty hovering outside my physical body that no one else could smell. I thought perhaps my body was diseased in some way, but my health was perfect. These happenings finally stopped after Jesus made his climactic appearance to me described earlier. I'd had about eighteen months of peace before the next incidents started.

Looking back, I should have recognized that something of question was hanging around. I would see Cypress, my most attuned cat, staring into space, looking disturbed. Shortly after that, I was abruptly awakened in the middle of the night to something invisible trying to suck the air out of my body. It felt like a tube had been placed over my lips and a vacuum was attempting to turn me inside out. It was noxious. I was not dreaming. As I jerked upright and began to spit in attempts to separate myself from whatever it was. Cypress, who had been sleeping under the covers next to me, sprang out growling and hissing. I had extreme nausea. I flipped on the light and remained sleepless the rest of the night.

This was not an isolated incident. It occurred many times. It got to the point that I was afraid to go to sleep at night for fear that I would be awakened by this incubus. I slept with an icon of Jesus, a photo of Paramahansa Yogananda and other sacred objects within my sight for protection. It did no good. I began to think someone was practicing black magic on me. I did all manner of crazy things I had read about or invented to safeguard myself. Salt around the bed does nothing!

The location where I slept didn't matter. I had the nightmarish episodes even away from home. One time I was visiting my parents for Thanksgiving and it happened in the room next to where they slept. I finally gained relief through work done with me by an intuitive who understands these issues, and the prayers for protection that I sent out at night before retiring. I also learned that I couldn't be lax in this respect. If I am, there seems to be an opening left for the ill-intended spirit to return. There have still been occasions when I've been awakened as before. But perhaps because I'm no longer as frightened by it, just angry that it shows up, its manifestation isn't full-blown and leaves as soon as I'm completely alert.

It seems to be an opportunist though, and looks for even slight avenues. The mystery of what those are remains unsolved by me. Even though I've written of dramatic times and esoteric events in this book to illustrate points, I am generally on an even keel emotionally. In fact, my life and consciousness have been such the past few years that I live in a state of continual gratitude. Just because I'm feeling my absolute best, that state doesn't act as a deterrent.

During such a time, I had been reading in bed before going to sleep. It was about 10 p.m. I reached over, turned out the light and lay down. I felt Cypress jump on the bed to join me. Immediately, she started hissing and spitting. A tussle was going on. I thought Cypress and Chloe, my other female, had gotten into it, there being jealousy between them. But no other cat was on the bed. I will also clarify here that while Cypress' personality is headstrong and rambunctious, her usual state of being is fairly quiet.

Suddenly, I felt something like a net coming down over my entire body trying to imprison me. I clawed off this unseen ensnarement. Throwing myself over on my side, I reached for the light, flipping it on. The clock showed only a few minutes from the time I'd shut off the light to go to sleep. Cypress was looking wild-eyed and I wasn't feeling so swell myself.

What was it about me that attracted such manifestations? This was the question that greatly disturbed and bemused me. It was particularly bewildering to me because I'd heard from more than one source in popular modern spiritual culture that the lighter the energy you carry, the more impossible it is for darker energy to reach you. I swallowed that doctrine for a period of time and felt frustrated with myself that I was carrying such negativity that drew the darkness to me like a magnet. Yet, I knew my strong intent for alignment with the Divine. I had also had manifestations of Jesus appear to me as well.

Was I mentally unstable? Hardly. Those who know me consider me to be one of the most grounded, sane people they know, in spite of my numerous mystical experiences. People regularly come to me to collaborate toward their own healing.

Then I began to realize that, hidden between the words in spiritual text, alluded to but not explicit, are mentions of the dark realm with which I had been dealing for years. From writings by mystics and stories about them, I finally recognized that when you open yourself to the spiritual path, you can't pick and choose. You *open* yourself—to everything. Even Jesus wrestled with demons.

It was particularly comforting to me to come across the writings of Kyriacos Markides. In some ways, he has likened himself to Carlos Castenada in that he is a participant observer. But his foci are the present-day mystics who live on the Greek peninsula of Mount Athos and his native island of Cyprus, dwelling under the auspices of the Greek Orthodox Church. He reports openly about the esoteric happenings that are part and parcel in the lives of these monks and hermits. One of the areas they periodically inhabit has to do with darkness similar to that I've described from my own life.

This fact validated for me my own dawning understanding, whose roots were first implanted in me through the hints that St. Teresa of Avila and others left. If we persevere on the path of purification and alignment with Divinity, it is possible that we may begin to leave the piddling trials brought about by mental convolution, or at least intersperse them with something else.

We enter another territory entirely. And its terrain is completely unknown and invisible to us. The code may be kept undecipherable.

Dangerous Liaisons

I remember being referred to once as "dangerous" by someone. She thought she should protect others from being exposed to my philosophy of conscious living. In one sense, she may be correct, at least certainly well intentioned. It can be a rough ride, particularly if you stand starkly on the path. Many may not be up to it. Those who are eventually find their way and don't really even have to look for it. Their own intent singles them out.

But what is really dangerous? Isn't it the places where some of us keep ourselves, perpetuating falsehoods, being horribly unjust and cruel to ourselves, and perhaps others? Is it risky to hold out the possibility of being completely in touch with your own heart?

The real threat is the doorway you don't go through for intent's purpose. The hazard is the obstinate glue of intention that keeps you stuck. *This* is the peril.

The recurring opportunity of Separation from one phase of the journey to another offers the points of departure for descent into the underworld and your own form of dark night. If you choose not to move into it, you may never find out how sleepy and foolish you have been.

It's only when we illuminate things that fear is disarmed. It's only by jumping into the void that we end up somewhere else.

Lose your footing.

Or—better yet—swan dive.

CHAPTER THIRTEEN

Unconditional Being

I had to go into the city that day and had left a little after nine in the morning. I'd been driving for about an hour thinking about the business that I was going to attend. I was feeling good about things in general when, out of nowhere, a deep sadness hit me. Anguish washed over me like a wave and brought tears coursing down my cheeks. Continuing to drive, I cried quietly for a few minutes until it finally subsided. But I was still left with the inexplicable sadness. Even so, I had a sense of its origins.

Late in the day, I returned home. Relaxing a bit after the trip, something kept urging me to meditate. My usual meditation time is first thing in the morning, not at night. Nonetheless, I followed the direction and slipped into the state. After clearing myself of the day, I checked in with a good friend, seeking out his energy body. Suddenly, I felt like I was sucked into a wind tunnel and was being taken somewhere. The strength of the pull was profound. I quickly backed out. Then I checked in on his dear wife, and felt her light, albeit very subdued.

And I confirmed for myself what I had indeed known to be true several hours earlier. A sweet man, a cherished friend, had released his body that morning. I spent the rest of the evening reminiscing about Homer and Marge, how our paths had crossed, what they'd come to mean to me. Even though they lived four hours south and we didn't see each other or talk that often, there was a deep connection that had nothing to do with time. I frequently spoke about them to others. One friend asked me once why I felt so strongly about them.

"They're the most authentic people I know." The words automatically slipped out.

"That's really saying something" He looked surprised.

Reflecting on it that night after my meditation, I thought to myself, I suppose it really *is* something. And I went on to a memory of walking the labyrinth Homer had made at their home. He'd dowsed my energy body for its size with copper rods before I'd entered and then again when I'd emerged. My field had grown immensely.

I brought up images of being at the retreat where we'd all met, and other times when we'd visited in each other's homes. I reviewed the time I'd stayed with them a few days and was going through a difficult period. Homer didn't say much. He just took me out to the back yard and suggested I sit in a structure called a Genesa Crystal made of iron rods placed in geometric patterns that was more than seven feet tall and nearly as wide. He told me it would make me feel better, but not to stay too long. I could see why. The energy it generated was powerful. The crystal gave some to me and I felt stronger.

I thought back to a few months before when Homer had sat at his dining room table dowsing a map of my property for water, using a pendulum and pencil as his tools. He'd been too sick to come do it in person. And I fast forwarded to just a few weeks prior when I could only stand at his bed, hold his hand and touch his head.

The next morning I went to my office where I had a phone, and found a number of messages awaiting me since the previous day. Yes. Homer had transitioned. I immediately called Marge, and shortly thereafter went down to stay with her for a while. When I sensed she would be all right by herself, I returned home knowing she also had a large local support network. Telephoning her a few days later, I found an amazing story waiting for me.

Some of her friends were involved in a prayer circle facilitated by a sensitive named Ellie. A session had been held as usual the day after I'd left. Midway through, one of Marge's friends asked to put her name in the circle since her husband had just passed. While other participants continued the process of adding those who needed healing, Ellie reported being distracted by a "short, bouncy, enthusiastic man." He was moving in progression around the table trying to get people's attention, tapping them on the shoulder. No one noticed him except Ellie, whose eyes were closed.

When she asked the friends at the far end of the table for the name of Marge's husband, they told her.

"Does he have a busy energy about him?"

"Yes!" Several people piped up.

"Homer is here then. I think he might have something to say."

Ellie later related that at this point she sensed shock coming from Homer.

"You know I'm here?" he cried.

"Yes, of course," she answered telepathically. "Is there something you'd like to say?"

"Tell them I'm alive! Tell them I'm alive!" With a burst of potency he got the message through, along with the gratitude that he'd been "heard" because he'd been trying so hard to contact people close to him. They hadn't received his messages. Then he indicated to Ellie that he would be at his memorial service that would take place in several days.

Homer went on to give some personal messages for Marge and then asked Ellie for permission to come again. Homer began to appear regularly to Ellie, and he often had some new friends with him. They offered wisdom teachings and reassurances to loved ones.

Did I have any doubts that the originator of these messages was indeed Homer? None. How otherwise could particular words and style of speaking that I recognized as Homer's come through a

163

woman who never knew him during his life on the material plane? There was a particular piece of counsel he sent that I found quite touching and comforting as any of us move toward rebirth. And the Rev. David Wilkinson read it at Homer's memorial service.

When I arrived at the service and sought Marge out, she said to me, "I told David you'd probably want to say something."

Of course I do, I thought to myself. But how can I put my sentiments into words? And how would I make it through what I wanted to express?

The service began. I watched Marge and heard her speak about her mate and their life together. I marveled at the strength of this woman. Homer and Marge were so attuned to each other they almost walked in lockstep. It was nearly impossible to even think of one without the other. I'd been deeply concerned about her wellbeing since Homer had transitioned. I witnessed there that she would ultimately be fine and felt immense relief.

Others spoke and then I somehow found myself standing at the podium. I hoped I'd adequately conveyed the rare opportunity I'd had to meet such down-to-earth, grounded people in the midst of esoteric pursuits. I talked about Homer's kindness, humility and "realness." I told a few stories, then gave the podium over to David.

David made a small joke about the gathering of the largest "woo-woo" crowd he'd ever seen in that locale. Everyone laughed, which brought some lightness to the event. He talked about his relationship with Homer and echoed what I had said. He jested about how he'd been a young man just starting his ministry when he'd met Homer and Marge. Now he had gray in his beard. Then, he began to read a message that Homer had sent through Ellie.

"...I'm more comfortable here now. It's not at all like I thought it would be. There are no words I could give you to describe it. It would be like trying to describe God. Words miss the fullness, the completeness of being here, so that any sense of here would be missed. Words are like describing a dot in a painting. Is it part of the painting? Yes, of course, but it is so little you would never know what the picture was from one dot. And this painting would have to be bigger than the whole world!

"Words are like using one grain of sand to describe your whole life experience on earth. It can't be done. It must be experienced. Understand?

"So anything I share is irrelevant for what I knew my friends would want to know. 'Details, Homer, give us details.' I can just hear them. What is relevant is that *I'm alive*. I hoped to be able to come through to give you peace, to let you know I'm okay.

"...I have to go now. Tell Marge I love her. But she needs to know and accept I'm okay and that I haven't left *her*.

"If you want to see if I can get through to you, *think* of me. Hey fellas! I'm a good-looking guy over here! I'm still a "shorty" but not so big. And I'm healthy. I'm okay. I'm really okay."

The pianist began to pound out "When the Saints Go Marching In." Everyone started to stand, clapping and singing. I was singing and moving my body, too. At the same time, tears were spurting out of my eyes as from the end of a water hose. But it was high emotion, not really grief—because I knew that, indeed, Homer lived.

All of a sudden, there he was! Homer's face hovered right before mine, grinning at me from ear to ear, making his round face even wider and crinkling his eyes up to mere slits. But I could see the lively sparkle! I could feel his great joy! And I clapped even louder.

Parting Thoughts

Divine guidance is ever present. We need only school ourselves in awareness. While the "burning bush" may present itself, it's more likely the way will be shown through words someone else may say, out of the blue, that resonate someplace deep inside. Or, a password may be sent through some cue in nature, or even the paranormal realm. Direction may come during meditation or some other reverie. And the real leap often comes through the dark night.

Look for what you are continually being shown. Open your ears. Be still. Listen.

Don't allow the clutter of your mind to distract you and hide the signals. Don't dismiss the Divine's guidance as just "natural phenomena" or tricks of your eyes or ears. Don't concede to your fears and close the door.

Life is the sacred cycle of Infinity, Life, Death and Rebirth. Some of us have fleeting memories of this perpetuation and keep it as we enter existence on this plane. This experiential knowledge gives deep comfort. While our feet walk this earth, we go through continuing iterations of the same. Some few of us can *see* what is beyond here. I can't for a minute believe it's dragons. For some of us, we have stories and faith that sustain us. We allow the understanding that all is merely a continuation of the sacred cycle of Creation.

Does it alleviate hesitancy, the reluctance to move on to other legs of the journey? That's a consideration of each individual alone. But if we also truly acknowledge the existence of All That Is, we cannot be apart from What Is. And to enhance each point of departure, we can ask the answers of ourselves.

What do I want to take with me?
What do I want to leave behind?
What appreciation exists for the learning I've had?
How will that learning shape my next life?

One time Don Américo talked about actors on a stage. He made a distinction. There are actors for society. There are actors for the Infinite. The stage actor merely practices the craft for the audience. Without an audience, that actor finds no meaning.

166

An actor for the Infinite acts no matter what. Any audience is inconsequential. While others may play a part and even benefit, the interchange is between the actor and the Cosmos.

And sometimes it is necessary to cocoon, to separate yourself from others, in order not to dilute your power, to gather your energies, to create the momentum that casts you through the next threshold.

I had made Jon's acquaintance through another friend. Each summer for several years running, Jon had been a fire lookout at Mt. Union, one of the highest points in North Central Arizona. In this isolated place, he had a small cabin in which to sleep and the fire tower from which to gaze upon mountain ranges all the way to the Mogollon Rim on a good day. The view and the ambience of the little abode and forest surrounding it were quite sublime as it was. But Jon was a deeply spiritual man. The pictures of saints and spiritual literature that were abundantly evident in both the cabin and tower, along with his own continual practices, imbued the environment with a palpable feeling of reverence, otherworldliness.

On a number of occasions, he had invited me to come up, any time I wanted, to stay for a few days. Toward the end of the summer I decided to take him up on his offer. My mind was confused about some things in my life and I sensed a deep urgency to go into retreat, to remove myself from my everyday environment to gain some clarity. What better place to do so?

When I called Jon he said, "Sure. Come on up. You'll have the place to yourself. I'm going down to the city for the weekend."

I was secretly delighted that I would be in solitude and grateful that I had somehow been provided that window of opportunity.

I arrived in late afternoon after having wondered if my car would actually make it up the primitive road. Jon welcomed me and showed me the ropes, how to conserve the water, how to climb and enter the fire tower. We sat up there for a while talking.

"What are you going to do once the summer is over?" I asked.

"I am so blessed. I don't know what I could ever do in exchange that would equal how I am divinely provided for. The next path will appear." He went on to tell me story after story about the unfolding of his good fortune.

At that point, I desperately needed to be told from an outside source what I already knew to be true. That's what I came to hear again and be reminded through Jon. Sometimes I forgot. I remembered that on my way up the mountain I had paused for a few moments and eaten some blackberries I had with me, then left the rest to the birds I saw in the underbrush. Traveling with the grace Jon described is like the birds unexpectedly delighted with the gift I had given them, not expected but easily discovered.

By the time he got ready to leave, a light rain had begun to fall and clouds were starting to silently move in and envelop the landscape. Before he turned to get in his car and head down the mountain, he gestured widely, taking in the surrounding forest, earth and sky. "Remember. Everything else is nothingness."

Then Jon was gone. The clouds had by now enfolded all. I could see only several feet beyond where I was standing in any direction. I was completely alone.

I went inside the cabin, having thoughts toward dinner. Choosing one from the many books Jon had, I carried my plate to the small table in front of the west window, which normally held a view level with, or above, far mountaintops. At the moment, I saw nothing but a solid white wall. And by now, the gentle rain had turned into a storm.

I'd picked up a thin volume written by Saint Thérèse de Lisieux, known as "The Little Flower." She hadn't lived past her nineteenth birthday. Even so, she had made a tremendous impact that still continued. I have always found it meaningful to read about the lives of the saints in their own hand. Through them, I am shown that they, too, went through struggles, wondered about their humility and worthiness. And many of them still delighted in some worldly things. Saint Thérèse was enchanted with dress, even though she wore a novitiate's habit!

I was engrossed in the book, but something in my peripheral vision was drawing my attention. I glanced out the window and couldn't believe what I saw. An immense fiery ball seemed to be hovering just beyond, in the ravine. I went out onto the porch to investigate. There it was—huge and blazing. How could the sun be coming to me in this way through the now torrential rains and impenetrable shrouding of clouds? I stood watching, awestruck, until the last remnants of this light finally disappeared.

Even though the storm was raging, I was compelled to sleep in the tower. I lugged my sleeping bag and a flashlight up the steep metal stairs, along with some water and Saint Thérèse's book. After arranging my bed for the night, I stilled myself and just watched the scene before me. From an altitude of around 8000 feet and the further height of the fire tower, I had a sense of being on top of the world. The clouds had raised enough that I could see the panorama of lightning dancing across the land. I'd never seen such a demonstration of raw power. Some strikes seemed too close for comfort and the thunderclaps vibrated the tower's cabin. But I just stood witness and found an uncanny metaphor in the stormy night to some of the inner turmoil that I'd brought with me to that place. Finding myself distracted and unable to read easily by flashlight, I lay listening to the sounds of thunder and raging wind for the longest time, feeling somehow perfectly safe. Peace was penetrating. I finally slept.

I opened my eyes very early the next morning. I heard no sounds of wind or rain. All was silent. I sat up. There were no clouds anywhere. Peace had come to the landscape. I could smell the fresh scent of washed pines coming to me through the small crack I'd left in one of the windows close by. My eyes came to rest on the mountain range toward the east. First light was appearing. I watched as the same fiery ball rose into view, smaller now, but its appearance just as profound to me. The cycle of renewal was complete.

When I turned to get up from my sleeping bag, I caught sight of a small plaque above Jon's worktable that I hadn't seen before. It was a picture of Jesus, arms outstretched. Underneath were the words "Lo, I'll be with you always."

Ultimately, the path is ours. Others support us along the way— even when it appears that they don't. But we have the final authority regarding the fall of our footsteps, the doorways we step through and the Dwelling Places we enter that can guide us to the eventual resting place of unconditional being.

What is a life?

It's the choice in every moment.

APPENDIX

THE RE-MEMBERING PROCESS

SPARKING   → → → → → →
Task: Waking up
Time: Present
Metaquestions:

Where am I?
What am I feeling?
What am I lacking?

↑
↑

Major sub-transition point

↑

RE-ENTRY
Task: Immersion
Time: Present, Future, Past
Metaprograms: Toward with Away From
Options with Procedure
Internal with some External
Metaquestions:
How do I return?
What gifts do I share?
What is the structure?
How do I implement?

↖

SEPARATION
Task: Unlearning
Time: Past, Future
Metaprograms: Away from
Internal
Metaquestions:
How did I abdicate?
Who am I <u>not</u>?
How do I serve myself?

↓
↓

Major sub-transition point

↓

SEARCH
Task: Widening choices
Time: Future
Metaprograms: Toward
Options
Internal
Metaquestions:
Who am I?
What are the possibilities?

↙

INITIATION
Task: Assimilation
Time: Present, Future
Metaprograms: Toward
Options with Procedure
Internal with some External
Metaquestions:
What are my gifts?
Where am I going?
What do I need?

THE RE-MEMBERING PROCESS

The edge of our reality depends on what we hold inside our minds as true and possible. We tend to recycle our lives—past, present, future all becoming one in the same—continually validating the filters through which we live. We continue to attract to us what we self-select through rote unconscious processes *until we don't*. When we don't, it's because something has awakened us to a wider life. With that wakeup call, different metaquestions are projected into the psyche from a place of higher wisdom. We begin to run *those* unconscious questions in our minds instead to attract to us the answers that will fulfill them. In alignment with the new metaquestions, a particular stream of metaprograms enact themselves to provide the thought and behavior orientations that serve us to step into the forest beyond the familiar compound where we used to live.

Mythologist Joseph Campbell named three phases to an unfolding: Separation, Initiation and Re-Entry. From an intimate viewpoint of my own journey and my work with others, I've seen that there are two other main developmental points to the path. While there is no prescription or prescribed schedule, I'm aware of these stages: *Sparking, Separation, Search, Initiation and Re-Entry.*

Many of us are on this path, in different phases and timetables. We are being propelled forward by the energetic momentum present with us in the world today demanding transformation now. If we're not involved and committed to the *Re-membering Process*, then we're still anesthetized, betraying ourselves and deceiving others.

The Sparking

Sparking is what awakens us from sleep and an unconscious life. It usually happens over a period of time, but can happen within an instant. It often occurs at mid-life, but if we're lucky or more conscious it happens much earlier. Even the Indian prince Siddhartha

Gautama, who later became the Buddha or Enlightened One, was once asleep behind the castle walls. It was only when he finally stepped outside the compound in which he lived that he began to see the wider world. So we all live within a container of some sort and are in a stupor to some extent. We can't escape it. It's part of the human condition. The questions are: how deep is the sleep? How big does the spark to awaken us have to be? What will jostle us out of the daily shuffle? What will cause our heads, bent over so intently eying our shoes, to rise up?

There are some of us who unconsciously decide, without really knowing why, to look up one day and *really* see the sky or a tree and the *Sparking* takes place. For others of us, it may be a seminar we attend or a book someone gives us at just the right moment. Only a month before, we wouldn't have heard the message or heard it in a lesser way. Then there are some who must be dynamited awake. These are the souls who have to experience a major crisis in their lives. For them, it's a significant illness, loss of a loved one or way of life that finally gets their attention. The important point is that no matter how we receive our *Sparking* it happens as it needs to for each of us. It's at that point we begin to be more aware of *how* we have been living our lives. In our semi-wakeful state, we slip ourselves these questions.

1) *Where am I?*
2) *What am I feeling?*
3) *What am I lacking?*

These are the unconscious mantras that run within our minds at this stage. A state of confusion exists that seeks to reach out into the fog and grasp onto explanations. *The task of the Sparking is to wake up.* We have an orientation to the *present*. Soon we may even become hyper-aware of the state of our lives. At this point, we transition to the next phase in the journey.

Separation

The task of Separation is un-learning. Once we begin to wake up, if we are truly going to continue on the journey, then leave-taking has to take place. It's a prerequisite of the course. We cannot travel a path toward authenticity maintaining a false life. The *Separation* phase is a major sub-transition in the evolution of *Re-membering*. Those who successfully carry it through find within them the great internal resource of courage to hold firm against the forces—internal and external—that struggle to re-establish homeostasis. It may be particularly dicey for individuals who are *externally motivated* and used to dependence on others for validation of their identity. What is required of *Separation* is a shift to *internal motivation*.

It's at this point that we begin to look at our lives and notice what really fits for us and what doesn't. Having been metaphorically asleep for so long, it was very easy for things to sneak in under the cover of night to nestle comfortably around and within us without our real knowledge—becoming a sort of prison containing our very self-expression. Through the conditioning process we all received messages, verbally and non-verbally, regarding what was "good" and "right" from our particular families of origin, schools and other societal institutions. Needless to say, "good" and "right" varied greatly depending upon our environments. In order to make sense of it all, the mind set up "look-outs" to filter out anything that didn't conform to the inherited paradigm. But during *Separation* the "look-outs" are somehow duped into guarding a decoy instead and an opening is provided.

During the *Separation* phase, we wonder where *we* went in all the previous years and what stranger is there instead. Operating in an *away from* metaprogram, we run these metaquestions about the *past* with a slight consideration of the *future* to move out of pain.

1) *Who am I **not**?*
2) *How did I abdicate?*
3) *How do I serve myself?*

In fine detail, we examine our jobs, relationships, homes—virtually everything in our lives that matter to us. As we see how we haven't been true to our own natures, discomfort and disorientation increase until a shift occurs. That movement may generate drastic change such as dissolving relationships, transferring career fields, or leaving a geographic location. There doesn't have to be a complete break with the pre-existing elements. However, discovery in this phase will allow the loosening of old beliefs, which will in turn begin to alter attitudes, feelings and behaviors to leverage possibilities to a new way of life. We are then brought to the next fork in the path.

The Search

The quest of the Search is to widen choices. During the *Search* we are looking at other perspectives and beliefs and trying them out. We seek to *explore options* and move *toward* them.

1) *Who am I?*
2) *What are the possibilities?*

We will find ourselves investigating areas that are new and different while we are immersed in the present. The promise of a fuller life may seem endless. So, we undertake things such as going back to school, inquiring into other careers, moving geographically, experimenting with new relationships, trying out diverse spiritual traditions or religions; many things to bring in additional data.

The Search can be as exhilarating as it can be scary. We may feel as though we've jumped out into space with no safety net to catch us. This is the time to call on the great faith. Otherwise, in fear, we would find ourselves clawing at the emptiness in attempts to head back to the compound. The dirty little secret no one told us before we took the leap is that there is really no turning back. Even if we would choose to turn our backs on the future, we're still different than who we were before. The future is guaranteed. It's just how easy or difficult do we want to make it. So we might as well press forward and happily complete the road rally. In the meantime, our minds may expand and contract. But if we pay attention, we will be directed by our intent to those things that fit for who we are at the core. We will know when we have arrived to the herald of our true home not by the logic of the mind, but by the response of the heart.

Initiation

When the heart is warm, it will feed the mind and further direct intent. After having been on the Search, the traveler comes to rest in the comfort of self-knowledge. *The undertaking of Initiation is assimilation.* We experience the *present*, move *toward* the *future*, employ the metaprogram *options with procedures* and ask:

1) *What are my gifts?*
2) *Where am I going?*
3) *What do I need?*

While many formal ceremonies exist the world over, the real *Initiation* starts and ends inside—where the self is finally proclaimed as whole and the wearing of masks no longer necessary. In this stage we know and appreciate the old life for what it was. We have made the decision to take the learning and discard the rest. We also intuitively know that there is a new life on the horizon, a deeper one that stands apart from the one that passed before. Having been on the trail for so long, we now stand apart from those who have not yet awakened. We also know we have something to teach—even if only by example. This is the cusp of a real beginning and the fog has nearly lifted. We can nearly see. We are readying ourselves for the journey back into the world. After a pause and full integration of who we now are and what gifts we have to share, we will re-enter those places from whence we came originally.

Re-Entry

The mission of Re-entry is immersion. Having tilled the ground with early questions of authenticity in relationship, spirituality, heal-ing, lifework and ecology and found some deeper realities, we come back to a world often not even yet aware of any need for evolution. But by holding the questions and the empty space where answers could exist, we will find ways to *Re-enter* and fill that void. We are still *internally motivated* but include some *external* reference; and consider the *future* for *options and procedures.*

    1) *How do I return?*
    2) *What gifts do I share?*
    3) *What is the structure?*
    4) *How do I implement?*

This is the final tasking of *Re-membering,* which furthers our own evolution as much or more than it may impact the environments in which we exist. If we don't come back, then we haven't completed the journey and we would remain floating somewhere without any real grounding.

This is the phase of our own transformation that can be equally as major a sub-transition as *Separation* was. It's not easy to enter places where what we have to give isn't always all that welcome. It can be frustrating and many of us will just want to give up and close ourselves off. But we can drop hints where we may. We can watch with our inner eyes for those who are ready for the *Sparking,* even if they don't consciously realize it. These are the people we can touch, even as we go deeper into our own transformation. These are the ones who will receive the gifts, even if we have to carefully parcel them out over time.

Patience and intent are indeed the by-words of *Re-Entry* that allow us to ask our own answers. Belief in ourselves and the possibilities of human potential cleave the way for what is to come. Questers first had to adhere to the strong *possibility* that the path was so. Then over time, the attractor of that energy created the magnet for events to align themselves to make the reality.

Excerpted from "The Questions We Live By" by Carla Woody, originally published in *Anchor Point: The Practical Journal of NLP*, September 2001. Reprinted with permission.

Note: Many books exist on the powerful change modality, Neuro-Linguistic Programming (NLP). I refer the reader to those books for in-depth discussions of NLP and its usage. For further information on NLP metaprograms, see Shelle Rose Charvet's book, *Words That Change Minds*.

Also by Carla Woody

Portals to the Vision Serpent

Calling Our Spirits Home: Gateways to Full Consciousness

Praise for

Portals to the Vision Serpent

by Carla Woody

"The search to find one's True Self is a journey that often challenges cultural preconceptions and assumptions. Portals to the Vision Serpent *takes this journey deep into the heart of the True People, delivering a story of longing and mystery woven like a story cloth between two worlds.*"

— Sharon Brown, Publisher, *Sacred Fire Magazine*

"Bloodlines are story lines. In Portals to the Vision Serpent, *Carla Woody invites the reader to explore the mysterious, ever-unfolding tale that each one must tell with our lives…one chapter at a time. Step into these pages. Invoke your true name. Re-member who you have always been.*"

— Jamie K. Reaser, author of *Sacred Reciprocity: Courting the Beloved in Everyday Life and Note to Self: Poems for Changing the World from the Inside Out*

"Portals to the Vision Serpent *is a transcendent spiritual adventure of a soul's inner and outer journey into the rainforests of Guatemala and Mexico, which brings awareness to the struggles of native people amidst the onslaught of cultural genocide.*"

— Matthew J. Pallamary, author of *Land Without Evil*

Praise for

Calling Our Spirits Home

by Carla Woody

Calling Our Spirits Home *is truly an enlightening guidebook for anyone looking for directions and tools for expansion, growth and transformation. Carla's gentle words invite everyone on a journey of complete healing and fulfillment. Help yourself with this book and you will find your way home.*
—Malidoma Somé, author of *Of Water and the Spirit*

This is a pleasing and easily read story that tells what we must know and what we need to become to live in this new millennium. It is a spiritual map that offers paths to success in life. Take this book as your map and you will find the way that is right for you.
—Dr. Gay Luce, Founder, Nine Gates Mystery School, author of *Longer Life, More Joy*

Calling Our Spirits Home *is a beautiful spirit song that gently gathers the dis-integrated, frightened parts of ourselves into the warm unconditionally loving wholeness of a mother's embrace…a celebration of life, mysticism and magic emerging as a blossom from the consciousness of humanity after centuries of growing beneath the compost of an unbalanced, materialist world.*
—Matthew J. Pallamary, author of *Land Without Evil*

Carla Woody writes a fascinating book in which she introduces thought provoking concepts. Her blend of metaphysics, myth and legend is simply amazing. The information in this book is multi-dimensional and gives the reader a chance to discern not only what the "journey" is as it applies to

consciousness; it also challenges the reader to do some self-examination...I applaud Woody for being artistic, challenging, and bold in writing this book, and including her personal experiences, lending credibility to her text.
—Metapsychology, The Mental Health Net

About the Author

CARLA WOODY has been mentoring people for more than twenty years, helping them make the leap to an un-prescribed life—consisting of an expressive prescription of their own making. In 1999 she established Kenosis LLC to support human potential through spiritual travel journeys and programs integrating Neuro-Linguistic Programming (NLP) and sacred world traditions. She founded Kenosis Spirit Keepers, a 501(c)3 nonprofit organization, in 2007 to help preserve Indigenous wisdom ways threatened with decimation. Carla writes books and articles related to spirituality, natural healing and advocacy of Native traditions. She is also a fine artist and makes her home near Prescott, Arizona. Please visit websites: http://www.kenosis.net and http://www.kenosisspiritkeepers.org. You are invited to follow her blog at http://thelifepathdialogues.com.

A final note from the author...

Thank you so much for reading this book. I hope you were touched in some way that enriches your own life.

If you think your friends would enjoy the book, I'd be honored if you'd let them know via Facebook and Twitter.

Your input makes a difference. I'd very much appreciate your feedback and read all reviews to let me know how I can reach readers in deepening ways. To leave a short review on Amazon go here: *http://tinyurl.com/kozvw3g*. If you're a reader on Goodreads, go here: *http://tinyurl.com/kbf5vyt*.

I extend an invitation to subscribe to my free ezine Kenosis Inspirations with articles, event announcements, reviews and more via these home pages: *http://www.kenosis.net* or *http://www.kenosisspiritkeepers.org*.

Many thanks again.

With all best wishes,

Carla